PRAISE FOR The 10-Minute Tidy

"Ten minutes is all it takes to start organizing and Shannon McGinnis shows you how. A great resource!" —PETER WALSH, Professional Organizer from TLC's hit series *Clean Sweep!*

"Common sense advice in *The 10-Minute Tidy* offers a clear path to eliminating clutter in your home. Shannon McGinnis' advice relieves stress and brings about change." —STANDOLYN ROBERTSON, CPO®, President of NAPO (National Association of Professional Organizers)

"This great little book is filled with common-sense tips to walk you step-by-step from overwhelm to order! Shannon makes it easy for you to get organized with *The 10-Minute Tidy.*" —PORTER KNIGHT, Professional Organizer, Speaker/Trainer and Author of *Organized to Last: Five Simple Steps to Staying Organized (book/dvd)*

"One of the hardest things to do on anybody's self-improvement list is to clutter-clear. Shannon takes this complicated deed, one which can profoundly impact the quality of your life, and turns it into a fun, manageable, and quick process. Pure genius! A must read for everyone!" —GABRIELLE ALIZAY, Author of *Feng Shui For The Rest Of Us*

"Shannon has a gift for organizing a wealth of information in bite-size amounts that are just right, so one can actually accomplish them!" —ALLYSON RAMAGE, EcoBroker®, Realtor®

"*The 10-Minute Tidy* is a guaranteed guide to feeling like a success in managing your home, work and life. Thank you, Shannon! You're a miracle!" —TALYA LUTZKER, Owner of Talya's Kitchen

The 10-Minute Tidy

The 10-Minute Tidy

*108 Ways to Organize Your
Home Quickly!*

SHANNON McGINNIS, CPO®

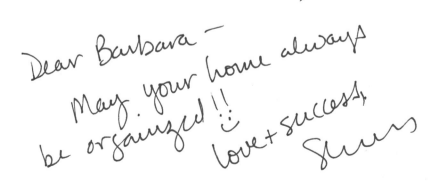

Dear Barbara —
May your home always
be organized !! :)
love + success,
Shannon

Organized 4 Success!
343 Soquel Avenue, Suite 414
Santa Cruz, CA 95062

ISBN-13 978-0-9800048-0-9
ISBN-10 0-9800048-1-0

Library of Congress Control Number: 2007907399

McGinnis, Shannon.
The 10-Minute Tidy: 108 Ways to Organize
Your Home Quickly!

Printed in the United States of America.

First Edition

To my clients, who have taught me so much.
May this book benefit you even more.

To my dear friends, who have always supported me
with love, laughter, food and dancing.
Thank you all so very much!

To Scott, without your love and support,
this book would not exist. I love and appreciate you!

Contents

Kitchen   33

Living Room   59

Bedrooms

Bathrooms

Closets 105

Office 119

Papers   143

Finances   159

Garage

How is it Possible to Tidy in 10 Minutes?

"The time for action is now.
It is never too late to do something."
CARL SANDBURG

We live in a fast-paced society and everyone is busy. Stress and overwhelm can override our ability to be more organized. However, I believe that you *can* become more organized, less stressed and have more time to do the things you love, if you spend just 10 minutes each day, or even every other day, implementing these 108 tidying tips! Tidying saves time and money in the long run, and you will be amazed at how being more organized will transform your life.

The 10-Minute Tidy is filled with clear-cut organizing tips that will help you to reinforce positive life habits in order to create greater ease, flow and fun in your life! The more open and spacious your home is, the more energy, love, money and happiness will flow to you and through you. By implementing these tidy tips, you will enjoy a renewed sense of beauty and appreciation in your home.

You can quickly and easily tidy your home—just use a timer

to keep your organizing projects manageable. Have *The 10-Minute Tidy* become a nightly routine for every member of your family! Play 10 minutes of the same music, around the same time each night, while everyone picks up their bedrooms and the common areas throughout the house (**Tip 42**). This fun family habit is an opportunity to tidy your home at least once every day. Every working parent knows how great it feels to wake up to a clean kitchen so make a nightly habit of doing all of the dishes (**Tip 24**). Even if you live alone, or don't have kids, implementing the tips in this book will help you be less stressed! When you have your most important items on your landing pad (**Tip 2**) everyday, you will know right where your keys are when leaving your home in a hurry. It's also important to only keep the things you love or use and get rid of the rest (**Tips 10** and **62**). Life is easier when you know where things go! Remember to celebrate and appreciate your accomplishments each time you complete a tidy tip (**Tip 108**).

Now it's time for you to implement these organizing tips, just 10 minutes at a time. Ready? Set? Go!

> *"Knowledge is of no value*
> *unless you put it into practice."*
> HEBER J. GRANT

Getting Started

"That which we persist in doing becomes easier for us to do;
not that the nature of the thing itself is changed,
but that our power to do [it] is increased."

RALPH WALDO EMERSON

You will learn how to be more organized by following the 108 tips in this book. By no means is it necessary to follow these 108 tips in any particular order. I recommend reading the Table of Contents or Index and selecting one tip or topic at a time. Start with what seems quick and easy to do and work up to the tips that feel more challenging to you.

Organizing is a habit and a process; by repeatedly using the organizing tips in this book, you will train yourself to stay more organized, automatically. For example, if you are always losing your keys, you can develop the habit of putting them in the same place (on your landing pad, **Tip 2**) each time you come home. Getting into the habit of implementing the tidy tips will help you feel better and think more clearly as you progress through the book. I invite you to enjoy the positive shifts that occur for you along the way.

One definition of clutter is: something that you haven't made a decision about. Clutter is the stuff set aside, piled on other things, or just randomly placed because you didn't know what to do with it. Make decisions about the things in your home, be intentional about where you put each item, and you will quickly eliminate chaos and create order in each room of your home and in your own mind.

Help children develop responsibility for keeping the entire house tidy by sharing with them the proper place to return objects; whether it's the remote control, their school books or their toys. Being organized allows everyone to stay in a rhythm of positive routine and consistency. Studies have shown that children increase their capacity to learn when their environment is clean, well organized and uplifting.

Reality TV shows like *Neat, Mission: Organization,* and *Clean Sweep* have introduced the concept of hiring a Professional Organizer to the general public. If you are feeling totally overwhelmed, know that there is help available to you and your family. As adults, we may be organizationally challenged; but by working with a Professional Organizer, you and your family will learn how to successfully implement organizing concepts. Organization provides a road map to help individuals and families cultivate project planning, time management, and other strategies to help everyone succeed at home, in school, in the workplace, and in life. Appendix C has information on how you can find a Professional Organizer near you or visit me online at **www.10minutetidy.com.**

Once you start to get organized, it's much easier to stay organized. Also realize that just as "Rome wasn't built in a day," you will not be able to clear years of clutter in a single day or even a month. Just begin with one tip right now. Simply open this book to any page to learn motivating, clutter-clearing solutions. The decision-making skills that you develop as a result of practicing these tips apply to every aspect of your life. Be consistent in developing your organizing habits and you will be amazed at how your home and your life will be transformed. Enjoy the process!

"Every day, in every way,
I'm getting better and better."
EMILE COUE

10-Minute Tidy
TIP 1

Take 10 Minutes to Visualize Your Clear, Organized Spaces

Yes, before you begin to do the physical organizing, it's important to visualize the clean, clear organized spaces of your entire home. The phrase that comes to mind is: "If you can see it, you can achieve it." So, before you begin your first 10-Minute Tidy, sit comfortably in your favorite chair and settle your mind.

Start by taking a deep breath and releasing all of the tension in your body. Take another deep breath and release all of the old stale air in your lungs. Take one more deep breath and settle your mind. In your mind's eye, imagine the way your home will look when everything is put away and you are surrounded by clean, clear, organized spaces.

What does each room look like? Imagine the clear horizontal surfaces of your kitchen, desk and floors. Feel the mood of each room as you are walking through. Smell the freshness of each space. Feel the joy in your body as you are able to glide easily and effortlessly throughout each room.

You can have this! You deserve clean, clear, organized spaces throughout your home.

Come back to your body in your chair knowing that in just 10 minutes a day, you can create this feeling of joy, peace and beauty. It can be easy; this book will provide you with simple steps to create the home you love to live in.

"It is a simple task to make things complex,
But a complex task to make them simple"
UNKNOWN

Create a Landing Pad

A "landing pad" is a phrase my client Jeff coined. A landing pad is the place where you can come into your home and drop your stuff. This is where you always keep your purse, fanny pack or wallet. Your cell phone plugs in, your keys hang up, and your pockets get emptied all while standing in the same place.

Your landing pad is a very personalized space that you create and designate as your own. Each person in the household will have a different landing pad. Your landing pad may be in the kitchen if that is close to where you enter your home. Someone else's might be in the office so that it's away from the common areas of the home. Also, each child needs his or her own hook to hang up their backpacks and coats.

Having a designated landing pad area is very important for creating new organizing habits. It is much easier to always put your keys on a hook if you can drop all the other things that are in your hands first. It's also faster to get out the door when you always go to the same spot for all your important items: keys, purse, sunglasses, and whatever else you take with you regularly. Create your landing pad now.

10-Minute Tidy
TIP 3
Clear Off Your Landing Pad

Once you have created your landing pad, you also need to clear it off so that you only keep what you need there every day. The key feature of the landing pad is that it is an open space for you to put things down when you get home. Therefore, this open space needs to be cleared from the extraneous items that might land there and stay too long.

If you walked in with your coffee mug from yesterday, and it's still on your landing pad, take 10 seconds to put the mug in the dishwasher. Or, if your children's landing pad is getting cluttered, remind them that it's important to put their things away in the proper place. Shoes or lunchboxes don't belong on a landing pad. Where are they supposed to go?

You may realize that you are not using your landing pad every day; now is the time to evaluate why. Is it located in an easy-to-reach area? Is it large enough for you to be able to empty your hands when you walk in the door? Perhaps you need a landing pad for household items and another for your work stuff. Determine why you are not using your landing pad and create one that would suit your needs better. You might even consider moving the furniture around!

A landing pad that you use everyday will save you lots of time and stress when you can find all of your most important daily items always in the same place. Train yourself to use your landing pad daily and I promise you, the mad dash out the door does get easier.

Consolidate Your "To Do" Lists

There are always things to do! Writing a list is a great way of keeping track of all that needs to be done. Perhaps you have multiple "To Do" lists. Now is the time to consolidate your lists onto one page. If you have various things to do, a small notebook with several sections could help you designate: Calls to Make, Events to Schedule, Items to Follow-up, and all the broad categories that are on your list.

I believe that every adult needs administrative time. Whether you work for yourself, someone else, or manage your household, everyone needs time to pay bills, make calls, and complete projects. I highly recommend that you schedule time to do the things you need to do on your lists. In 10 minute increments of focused, productive time, you can complete items on your To Do list.

A mantra that I suggest is: "If it takes less than one minute, do it now." Remember this when you are recopying items to complete from one To Do list to another. Rather than rewrite "Write Sally a Thank You card," take the time to do that right now. It takes about a minute to write a quick thank you note.

You may even want to send a card online so you can save yourself the trip to the mailbox and the stamp. It really is amazing how many tasks you can get done in about a minute.

Consider asking others to help you if you have something on your To Do list that hasn't gotten done yet. Perhaps you could have a conversation with a friend about what your resistance is to this task. You can also ask your friend to check in with you to ensure that you are accountable for getting it done.

"Ideas won't keep; something must be done about them."
ALFRED WHITEHEAD

Getting Started

Write Your
"Top 5 Things To Do Today" List

It is easier to get your tasks accomplished when you prioritize your day. Create a "Top 5 Most Important Things To Do Today" list and post it somewhere that it will remind you to stick to your priorities. Perhaps you have picked an area that you want to focus your 10-Minute Tidy on today. Be sure that it is on your Top 5 list.

You may write down more than 5 things to do today, but be sure to prioritize the items in order of importance. This simple time management systems works! Have you ever heard of the 80/20 rule? This is a principle known as Pareto's Law, which states that 80 percent of your effectiveness will come from achieving 20 percent of your goals. That's why it's important that you focus on the most important items on your "Top 5 Things To Do Today" list.

"We are what we repeatedly do.
Excellence, then, is not an act, but a habit."
ARISTOTLE

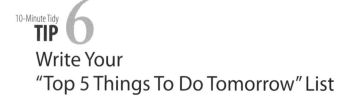

Write Your
"Top 5 Things To Do Tomorrow" List

At the end of the day, it's important to review what got done and decide what the priorities are for tomorrow. It is easier to get things done when you prioritize what you want to accomplish each day. Create a "Top 5 Most Important Things To Do Tomorrow" list at the end of the day and keep it somewhere where you will see it early in the morning. This list will remind you to stick to your priorities. Then your "Tomorrow" list effortlessly becomes your "Today" list when you return.

"Great opportunities are like raindrops.
They only come around every once in a while,
And they can easily slip through your fingers."
UNKNOWN

TIP

Schedule Self-Care Appointments

On every airplane flight we are reminded to put on our own oxygen mask first, before we help our children or others around us. Self-care is so important, yet sometimes we need to be reminded to do this. Now is the time to schedule one or two self-care appointments.

Self-care can look and feel very different for each person so take a moment to think of what would be fun for you to do. Your options are endless but here are a few suggestions:

♦ go for a walk with a friend

♦ have a fancy lunch date

♦ get a massage

♦ have a pedicure or manicure

♦ plan a few hours to be home ALONE

Health-care appointments are also necessary so consider scheduling an eye exam, teeth cleaning or a mammogram. Take care of yourself.

Schedule and Use
Your Gift Certificates

Another part of being disorganized may be that you have many gift certificates all around your home or office and don't know where they are or when they expire. As soon as you find a gift certificate, call or schedule a time to take advantage of this great gift someone gave you. Even if you have to schedule time to go to the mall to visit a particular store, take the time to schedule this now so that you don't miss a great opportunity.

You may also want to create a place where you put all of your gift certificates that you are not able to redeem right away. One option is to keep them in the kitchen in your recently organized coupon holder (or accordion check file, see **Tip 21**). Or you may create a file labeled Gift Certificates. Keep them all together in a place where you can easily find them when you want to take advantage of a free meal, round of golf, or a great massage!

Set All the Clocks in Your Home to the Same Time

How annoying is it when you get ready in the bathroom and then go into the bedroom to get dressed and dash to the kitchen to grab coffee and some breakfast only to realize you have been basing your schedule on clocks that are all set at different times? This is so frustrating when you are running late and you look at the atomic time clock on your cell phone and realize it is more than a few minutes off from the other clocks in your home.

Take your cell phone, which is linked to the atomic time clock, and go room by room resetting all alarm and wall clocks. Also check everyone's watches so that they are also set to the exact same time as everything else in your home. Finally, synchronize all of the clocks in each of the vehicles.

Celebrate this message to the universe that everyone will easily be on time now!

Create a Donation Bag and Put Five Things in It

If you are reading this book, you probably have at least five items that you could donate to someone else. I encourage you to create a donation bag and keep it centrally located in your home. The front hall closet, the laundry room, or in the garage are all possible places for the family donations bag. Once everyone knows where to put the clothes that don't fit, the books they have read, or the toys they no longer play with, the donation bag will fill up quickly. When it is full, put it in your car to be dropped off at the nearest donation center, church, or homeless shelter so that others may benefit from the items that you no longer need.

If you have larger items to donate, consider contacting the

♦   Salvation Army **www.salvationarmyusa.org**

♦   Goodwill **www.goodwill.com**

♦   St. Vincent de Paul **www.svdpusa.org**

for pick up. It is wonderful to offer to others the things you no longer use. See **Tip 11** for possible tax benefits.

Itemize Your List of Donations

It is of great value for you to itemize your donations because you may be able accumulate a wonderful tax deduction by the end of the year. Check with your tax advisor to determine whether an itemized list of donations would qualify you for a tax benefit. It is a good idea to itemize your donations anyway, because your situation might change mid-year so even though you don't qualify now, you may later in the year.

If you decide to itemize your donations, make a list of all of the items in each load of donations that you take to the donation center. Your family can even help you create this list if you have a clipboard, pen and paper next to your bag of donations. Every time you have a full bag be sure that you have listed the items you are donating before you drop it off. Be sure to get and keep the receipt from the donation center.

Using your list of donations, you can hand write an estimated value next to each item. The donation values are approximately 25% of the original cost of the item. Your list should also include how many of each item (i.e. 6

pairs of women's dress pants) and the condition they are in (new, good or fair). The Salvation Army website also has a general valuation chart, **www.salvationarmyusa.org** (Donate-Receipts-Valuation Guide).

It is also very easy to use the It's Deductible™ program in Turbo Tax™ for inputting this data, **www.turbotax.com**. You select the items donated, insert the quantity and quality, and the It's Deductible™ program gives you a list of the tax-deductible value of each category for that donation. Attach your receipt from the donation center, the printout from It's Deductible and file it with your other tax return items.

For donations of over $600, it is also advisable to take a photo of the items (in piles, bags, or boxes) to substantiate your contributions if you ever need to prove it for tax purposes. Print the donation photos and keep the printouts with the receipt and itemized list from It's Deductible™. Enjoy saving money while getting rid of the stuff you no longer want!

Take a Load to the Donation Center

Now that you have the full bag, box or carload ready to be donated, be sure to get a receipt when you drop it off. To find the nearest donation center to your home, it's easiest to look up 'Thrift Shops' in your local phone book's yellow pages.

So many people will benefit from the clothes, books, housewares, electronics, and sporting goods that you and your family no longer need. Enjoy offering all of your unwanted possessions to others as an abundance of generosity.

Homeless shelters and women's centers are wonderful places to donate where the recipients get to choose what they need for free. I feel truly blessed that we live in a country of such abundance that we can offer our possessions to others freely. Hopefully you, too, will feel this blessing the next time you take a load to the donation center.

> *"Don't be afraid to give up the good for the great."*
> **KENNY RODGERS**

Look Up Freecycle.org for Your Local Area

Freecycle.org is an amazing website resource for you to either get what you need for free or offer what you have to someone else for free. Freecycle.org has local groups that anyone can join. There are always amazing items being given away for free. You usually have to arrange pick up as there is no delivery service.

I encourage you to use the freecycle.org network to offer others whatever you do not want and/or cannot take to a donation center.

However, I caution you to be aware of taking in too many items from freecycle.org. Remember the goal is to stay organized and to only keep the things you love and the items you use. This is not an opportunity to acquire more junk. If you can't resist the temptation to get a piece of exercise equipment for Uncle Bob, just be sure to freecycle it back into the community if he hasn't used the new acquisition in three months!

Check out this amazing resource, **www.freecycle.org!**

Gather Items to Be Returned

Do you have something that needs to be returned to someone? Whether it is a library book, serving bowl, or DVD, there is probably something that needs to get out of your house and be returned to the proper owner. It feels great to return an item to the store for a refund. Credit on your credit card or cash back in your pocket for returns is instant gratification.

During this 10-Minute Tidy, gather the items that need to be returned and take them out to your car. You may also want to schedule a time to run these errands. Or, you may be able to incorporate a return while on another errand. For instance, you may be able to give a serving bowl back when you pick up your kids at school. Books for the library can be stored in a particular book bag so that they are easy to identify. Videos can be returned on the way to or from the grocery store.

Stores appreciate it when you bring a return or exchange item in their store bag. They also often require a receipt. Don't despair if you can't find the receipt; stores will often offer an exchange rather than a refund if you can not find the receipt.

You may also have things that need to be "Returned to Sender."

For example, Netflix DVDs, impulsive Internet purchases, or something in the wrong size are all "Return to Sender" items. It is important to schedule a time when you can ship these parcels back to their sender. Many large department, grocery, or drug stores also have Mailing Centers, which are open much later than the post office so you have more options for late night returns.

It feels great to be able to get several of these mundane tasks accomplished. You have freed up both physical and psychic space by completing all your returns. Now you might even have more money in your pocket or have reduced your credit card bill! Congratulations!

Purchase Organizing Containers

Sometimes you need just the right container to deal with the stacks of stuff to be sorted. If you know where you want to store the items you are sorting, measure the shelves or space so that you buy the perfectly sized containers that will best fit in that area.

There are thousands of containers to choose from. Rubbermaid™ makes some of the best, **www.rubbermaid.com**, in my opinion. The Container Store™, **www.containerstore. com** and Space Savers™, **www.spacesavers.com** have a wide variety of organizing supplies that can be purchased online.

Your larger hardware stores will also have a variety of containers that you can buy locally. Plus, department stores such as Target and Wal-Mart™ have storage containers in the housewares department.

Don't buy too many containers before you have sorted your clutter or at least measured the area where you want the containers to be stored. Measure the depth of the closet, the height of the drawer and the length of the shelves to be sure that each container fits in that particular area.

You can then calculate exactly how many of the same container can be stacked and stored in that space. Budget Closet™ actually designs their cabinets specifically so that the most common containers will fit side by side and easily slide onto the shelves without bumping the hinges. Fantastic!

Gather Items for the Dry Cleaner and Put Them in Your Car

Does your dry cleaning end up draped over the back of a chair or heaped in the corner of your closet for months? Create a designated bag for dry cleaning and always have that bag hanging in one specific place. Perhaps you keep the dry cleaning bag in the master bedroom closet so that the shirts and blouses that get taken off can go right into this bag. You could also keep your dry cleaning bag in the laundry room so that certain pieces of clothing go into the bag when the laundry is sorted. Pick one place and have your dry cleaning always go into the same bag.

Once the bag is full, take the items to be dry cleaned and put them in your car for immediate drop-off. If you have a regular weekly routine, it saves you lots of time and energy to quickly grab the bag to drop off at the dry cleaners.

Consider supporting a dry cleaner that is conveniently located for you or one that is environmentally-friendly. Yes, there actually are dry cleaners that are conscious about how their products affect the environment. Inquire as to which one is 'green' in your local area.

Collect and Take Out
All the Recycling

In California it is easy to recycle because we have curbside recycling pickup. Many other states are also offering recycling services with their garbage pickups. Check with your local waste service to learn how you can participate. Often, the recycling bins are free—you only pay for the "waste" bin. Another money saving tip: recycling allows you to have a smaller waste bin, which costs less!

It is important to recycle as much as possible so that less ends up in the landfills. There are websites, such as **www.earth911.org**, that assist you in finding a recycling center near you. Collecting your bottles, cans, mixed papers (junk mail, newspapers, magazines, printer paper), and cardboard allows that much more to be broken down and reused.

Donations are also an act of recycling. Take your gently used clothes, household items, and electronics to local donation centers rather than throwing them away.

There is also a collection return reward for many types of bottles. Sarah collects her recycling for her daughter to take to school as a fundraiser. It's a great way for kids to learn to be environmentally responsible as well as make some extra money.

Having recycling bins in your kitchen, garage and office allows you to easily collect all of the household recycling and take it out in less than 10 minutes. This could be an easy task to delegate to an older child (see **Tip 18**). Enjoy recycling!

"If you can give your son or daughter only one gift, let it be enthusiasm."
BRUCE BARTON

Collect All Trash
and Empty the Shredder

An older child can easily collect all the trash from every room in the house in less than 10 minutes. One simple solution is to start with the kitchen trash and go around to each room and dump the trash into the kitchen trash bag. Be sure every bedroom and bathroom has a trash can, as this allows no excuses for anyone to leave used tissues on the floor or under the bed.

When in the office, be sure to empty the shredder into the trash as well. Shredded paper strips or bits can not normally be recycled. Check with your local recycling service to determine if they accept shredded paper. Shredded paper usually contains staples and other foreign matter, especially if you shred credit cards and CDs. I feel great about emptying the shredder into the trash because it is already pre-composted material.

Speaking of compost, shredded paper is contaminated with a variety of inks so you many want to reconsider emptying the shredder into your compost bin.

Type Housesitting Instructions for Your Home, Family and Pets

You will probably have a baby-, house- or pet-sitter sometime during the year. If you have typed-up instructions with all the important phone numbers, addresses, and locations of specific items, you will save yourself lots of time and stress. Having a general document that you can easily edit and print out is a great timesaver.

In about 10 minutes, you can compose an instruction sheet of who to call and their number. You may also want to include where to find the medicine and pet food, and what the neighbors names and numbers are for any occasion when someone is going to be staying at your home and you won't be there.

You can find general babysitter sheets on the Internet and then customize whatever information you need to share with your babysitter or housesitter. Be sure to include where the remote controls are, how your main electronic components work, where inside and outside light switches are, and how to contact you. An instruction sheet is an easy solution to have your home, pets and family well taken care of when you are away.

Clear the Floor in the
Messiest Room in Your House

This could be the busiest 10 minutes ever, but I encourage you to turn the music up and get busy clearing the floor of the messiest room in your home! Bring several trash bags with you and designate ones for Trash, Recycling, Donations, and Things to Keep. Your "Things to Keep" might even be separated into what belongs in different rooms.

You will be amazed at how quickly you can tidy the messiest areas and how long 10 minutes will feel. Don't stop for even 10 seconds until the timer goes off. When the timer rings, dump the trash in the trash can, the recycling in the recycling bin, put the donations in your car, and return the things you want to keep to their proper places.

You can be more organized and less stressed in 10 minutes or less! Be sure to go back and admire your cleared floors. You may even be inspired to vacuum.

Kitchen

"If you can organize your kitchen,
you can organize your life."
LOUISE PARRISH

The kitchen is the heart of the home and everyone uses it everyday. People love to congregate in the kitchen, snacking, talking and sharing their day. It is important to have a clean, clear kitchen so that it's easy to prepare delicious meals.

You may be wondering how you can possibly tidy the kitchen in 10 minutes, but you actually can. Here are 14 ways that you can systematically sort, purge and tidy the kitchen in 10-minute increments. Your kitchen might have four to 20 drawers in it, but if you can sort and clear one or two drawers in 10 minutes, the task of organizing the kitchen is not overwhelming.

Have everyone in your home help you keep the kitchen clean and tidy by doing the dishes every day. Clean-up supplies within easy reach make it easy to wipe up spills, counters, the sink and stove. You could even label drawers and shelves so that the proper items get returned to their designated places. This can be fun, are you ready? Get set. Go!

Sort, Purge and Organize Your Coupons

Almost every kitchen has a drawer or area where the coupons get stuffed. Coupons are a great way to save money. I have saved over $43 on a $112 grocery bill while using coupons, but coupons are only valuable if you use them. Most of the time they expire before they get redeemed. Now is the time to sort, purge and organize your coupons.

I recommend a 13-pocket, half-size, accordion file folder, called a check file. These can be purchased at most office supply stores for less than $5 and are typically plastic. The check file has pockets that can be labeled according to your coupon categories. Suggested labels are: Food, Cleaning Supplies, Pet Products, Car Wash, Car Repairs, Video, Pizza, Restaurants, Menus. There will also be room for additional categories such as: Phone Numbers, Home Repair Info, and Babysitters.

Once you decide on your categories, it's easy to sort your coupons into each labeled section. Be sure to check the expiration date on each coupon. Any expired coupons can be recycled and the current ones can be filed.

Some "big box" stores such as Bed Bath & Beyond® will accept their expired coupons so you may want to keep all of your coupons for these types of stores.

You may want to keep your coupon holder in your car if it is more convenient for you to use them when you are out doing errands. You could also have two of these check files; one in the kitchen for pizza and take out menus, the other in your car with the grocery and car wash coupons for quick and easy use.

How much money can you save using coupons?

Sort, Organize
and Clean Out a Drawer

Every kitchen has a variety of drawers and sometimes it feels like most of them have turned into junk drawers. Now is the time to sort one drawer at a time. Since the notorious "junk drawer" can seem overwhelming, I've dedicated the next tip (**Tip 23**) to just organizing the junk drawer. This 10-Minute Tidy focuses on all the other drawers in the kitchen, one at a time.

Perhaps you want to start with the silverware drawer since this is the one that gets used every day. Hopefully you are using a silverware holder that easily accommodates all of your daily utensils. I love the expanding silverware trays that fill the entire drawer. You can purchase these at most large household supply stores. They are also great in another drawer for your serving and cooking utensils.

When cleaning out a drawer, you may want to dump the entire drawer out onto the counter so that you can clean the bottom of the drawer. Perhaps you want to put in new contact paper or line the drawer with something to prevent the organizing tray from sliding around when the drawer is opened and closed.

Once the drawer is wiped out and the silverware tray or your organizing bins are in place, decide what you want to put back in. Only keep the utensils that you use. Anything that has been chewed up by the garbage disposal or melted on the stove is trash. There is nothing worse than eating something smooth and creamy like ice cream and then having the jagged edge of the spoon scrape your lip! Throw those away right now! They cannot be fixed and unless you remove them from the kitchen, they are just going to be kept in circulation.

Also, evaluate how many of each item you really need. How many spatulas does your family use in a week? How many potholders do you really use per meal? Why keep more than two sets of tongs unless you entertain often? Just keep the items you love to use. I have an adjustable can opener from my Gram that I absolutely love, so even though the paint is peeling off the handle, it works just as well as it did 40 years ago.

So, keep what you love to use; throw out anything scraped, melted, or broken, and donate all the extras. You will have an organized kitchen, one drawer at a time.

Organize the Junk Drawer

Most kitchens have a household junk drawer where all the odd items end up that don't have a home. This is where the flashlights might be with the screwdrivers and extra picture hangers. When you decide to tidy this drawer in 10 minutes, first decide what actually should be kept in the drawer and what can be relocated to the garage, basement, or laundry room.

The best way to start may be to dump out the drawer and wipe it clean. This is the ideal place for drawer organizers. Use separate drawer organizers for batteries, hardware, and tools. See exactly what you want to keep in here and what actually fits. A hammer may take up too much room and so it might be better located in the garage. If everyone in the house knows where the hammer is stored, then they are also more likely to return it to that place in the garage rather than throw it in the junk drawer again.

There are also plastic trays that you can buy that have compartments of various sizes. Using this type of drawer organizer, you can decide if you want to separate batteries by size: AAA, AA, C, D, others. Plastic trays are also great to separate household hardware such as screws, nails, picture hooks, and thumbtacks. This type of adjustable tray can be purchased at your local hardware store in the household section.

Your household junk drawer may be cluttered with keys or sunglasses. Look at all of the sunglasses to see if they are scratched or out of style and donate all the pairs that you no longer wear. Keep your collection down to a reasonable number; otherwise you have too many choices that slow you down when trying to get out the door.

Keys are often a loose item that end up in the junk drawer. Take the time to check the loose, extra keys with the doors, filing cabinets and bike locks in your home. Check any locking china cabinet, jewelry box and safe before throwing away extra keys. You would know by now if there were something that you weren't able to get into. If you haven't used any of those keys in a long time, chances are that you won't suddenly need to.

A junk drawer is great, but it's even better when you can easily find exactly what you need in it!

Wash Dishes or Empty the Dishwasher

It is a simple thing to do and yet one that we resist so much! I am amazed at how much better I feel when the kitchen is free of dirty dishes. Somehow a dish drain of clean dishes doesn't bother me as much as a pile of dirty ones. Do you feel the same way?

For immediate gratification, set your timer for 10 minutes and wash as many dishes as you can! You can also easily load the dishwasher in 10 minutes. If the dishwasher needs to be emptied, unloading the dishwasher only takes a few minutes and then it's ready for refilling.

For the pots, pans, knives, and cutting boards that you don't put in the dishwasher, washing as many as you can during the remaining 10 minutes will go quite quickly if you race yourself or make a game out of it. This is a great way to enroll children in the process too. Kids can race to see who empties the dishwasher and who clears the table faster. Just be sure that there are penalty points for broken dishes.

Notice how much better you feel when the kitchen is clear of dirty dishes piling up on the counters or in the sink!

Match Up All Plastic Storage Containers

Oh, the chaos of plastic storage containers! This could be one of the most satisfying areas to organize in your entire home! Most kitchens have a drawer or cabinet where these containers get thrown, never to be matched up again. Today is the day! Now is the time! This is actually quite fun if you think of it as a puzzle.

First, decide what your strategy is. Do you want to only keep one kind or brand of storage container? Do you want to store the glass ones somewhere else? Perhaps you want to get rid of everything and start over with a new, color-coded, complete set. If this is the case, I would recommend recycling as many containers and lids as your local recycling program will accept. Then wipe out the area and start with a clean slate.

Pam uses the "as-seen-on-TV" plastic container system that has all the same lids with 3 different sized containers, all stored on a rotating base. This is such a great solution, I bought one for myself at Kmart™ for about $20. It fits in cabinets easily and I love it!

If you want to continue to use the storage containers that you have, then start by shape. First match up all of the rectangular containers. Then move on to the square containers. Next are the round containers and there are usually more of these: bowls, cups, and to-go mugs. Again, be realistic about how many you need of each and only keep the ones that have matching tops and bottoms that you will use.

Any extra tops or un-matched bottoms can be recycled or thrown away. Plastic storage containers that have been stained, melted or scraped should be recycled or thrown away to prevent bacterial contamination.

Enjoy being able to easily find the matching top and bottom to your plastic storage containers from now on and repeat this 10-Minute Tidy as needed!

Go Through Cabinets and Throw Out Chipped, Cracked, or Broken Serving Ware

Everyone, everyday, uses plates, bowls, and glasses in the kitchen. What kind of message are you sending to yourself and everyone else if you are serving food on cracked plates? Bacteria can grow in those crevices and unless your dishwasher washes at very high temperatures, you may also be serving millions of bacteria in cracked serving ware. The universe grants you full permission to throw away or recycle all chipped, cracked, or broken serving ware.

Start with the cabinets you use most often. The everyday dishes may be chipped or cracked due to their daily use. Once you have sorted out the dishware you use most often, sort though the cabinets you use less frequently.

You may need a stepstool to sort the back, top shelf of a lesser-used cabinet. This is probably where the bowls or mugs are lurking and collecting dust that you haven't seen since before your kids were born. These are the ones that you may be able to eliminate most easily. If any item is broken, it's trash and should be thrown away. If you just don't like it anymore, then donate it. The age-old adage is "One person's trash is another person's treasure."

Create "Kids' Kitchen Stuff" Accessibility

Once kids start to eat on their own, you can train them to get their own plates, cups, bowls and utensils. Designate a drawer in the kitchen just for their stuff. The drawer (or basket) must be low enough for them to see and reach into. Then they can take out their own plate and cup for a snack or help you unload the dishwasher and put their own serving ware away.

A water dispenser that children can reach empowers them to help themselves. Therefore you have more time and less "Mommy, can I have a cup of water?" requests! Remember, if it drips or spills, it's only water.

You might also want to have a place where the kids can easily access rags or old towels to clean up their spills. Toddlers seem to want to help clean up. If you allow them to do it on their own, who knows? Maybe when they're teenagers they will still remember where the rags are kept and clean up their own messes!

Organize and Label
the Pantry

Depending on how large your pantry is, this may take more than 10 minutes. I spent 3 hours organizing a client's pantry because it was packed with things in front of things! If you can't see what's in your pantry, chances are you have forgotten about it and that most of those items along the back walls are expired.

Set your timer for 10 minutes and sort through just one area of your pantry. Expired food should be thrown out, not donated or eaten. Food expiration dates are posted for a reason. The chemicals in food begin to denature and break down so the ingredients just aren't the same anymore. Food should be regarded as spoiled if the expiration date has passed. Any expired food you throw out is just a reminder of the importance of regularly organizing and taking inventory of what is in your pantry.

Store cans, bottles, and bags in just one layer, or have tiered shelves so that you can see the labels of each container. I also recommend that you label the shelves so that everyone else in your home can put away or quickly find each category: pasta, sauces, spices, baking supplies, cereal, and pet food.

Have fun and get creative with all those long lost ingredients you didn't know you had in your pantry. Be generous and donate anything you don't think you or your family will enjoy before the expiration date. This could be a fun area to have your kids help you organize.

"If we're not willing to settle for junk living, we certainly shouldn't settle for junk food."
SALLY EDWARDS

Kitchen

TIP 29

Purchase or Install
Extra Storage Options

Do you have enough storage space in your kitchen? There are many easy solutions to create additional storage space. First you need to decide what you need more room for. Have you sorted all of your cabinets and drawers and really evaluated whether or not you want to keep everything? If you have eliminated all the extras, then it's time to get creative about what you want to do to expand your storage possibilities.

If you are wanting easy, inexpensive solutions, a "lazy susan" might just do the trick in those hard to reach cabinets. I recommend using a "lazy susan" for all your oils and vinegars so that you can see and grab whichever one works best for that meal. I also encourage my clients to either install spice racks on the wall or use a multi-tiered shelf in a cabinet close to the stove so that they can see the label of each spice bottle and easily reach it when cooking.

There are a variety of door racks that can be installed for extra pantry space. Just be sure that the door will support the additional weight, depending on if you are going to store tea or canned goods there. Pull-out shelves are great solutions for the deeper cabinets where the back items are either hard to see or out of reach.

If you would prefer to have someone else install additional kitchen storage space for you, there are many companies who specialize in this. Budget Closet™, Closet Factory™, California Closets™, Rev-A-Shelf®, Shelf Conversions®, and The Pull-Out Shelf Company® are just a few companies who install kitchen systems.

I highly recommend that you invest in the kitchen to make it easier to use and more enjoyable to be in. Everyone in your home uses the kitchen every day.

TIP 30
Organize the Spice Jars

The spice jars always seem to end up disorganized unless they are stored in a way that is easy to maintain. Spice racks, "lazy susans" and tiered shelves allow you to see the labels of each jar. Your 10-Minute Tidy of the spice jars involves taking all the spices out from where you store them, evaluating what you have that you will actually use, and then deciding which system will best support you (and the rest of your family) to keep the spice jars in order.

How do you use your spices? It's rare that you use all of your spices in the same meal. Therefore you may want to group the spice bottles in categories of sweet, savory, Italian, curries, etc. I actually use small drawer organizers with my spice bottles in them so that when I am baking, or making oatmeal, I can pull out the cinnamon, nutmeg, ginger, and cloves all at once. This is a quick and easy storage solution for me since the cabinet I keep my spices in is too narrow for a lazy susan. I also love the 4 ounce, round magnetic tins with clear lids that stick on the fridge or stove hood. Not only can you easily read the labels, but because the lids are clear, it is easy to see how much is inside.

If you are storing your spices in a way that you cannot read the labels, consider re-labeling each spice jar on the lid or in a different location so that you can easily identify each one.

Cooking is fun and having your spices stocked and organized will allow the creative process to be that much more enjoyable. Bon appetite!

"Some people like to paint pictures, or do gardening, or build a boat in the basement. Other people get a tremendous pleasure out of the kitchen, because cooking is just as creative and imaginative an activity as drawing, or wood carving, or music."
JULIA CHILD

Kitchen

Clear Off the Front, Top and Sides of the Refrigerator

Everyone goes into the fridge every day and at some point we become blind to the clutter that is on the outside. Depending on how cluttered your fridge is, this 10-Minute Tidy may be done in multiple stages.

Begin with the top of the fridge. When was the last time that anyone had a bird's eye view of this area? Get up on a chair or step stool and take a look. You will probably be shocked at the amount of dust on top of the refrigerator.

What is lurking way in the back? Sort what you want to keep, donate or throw away. What actually *should* be stored on top of the fridge? Do you have cabinets above the fridge that you haven't opened since you moved in? You may want to peer inside. Did you know that you actually don't have to store anything in the cabinets above the fridge? You could actually have empty cabinets and no one would know.

What is stored on top of the fridge is highly visible and also likely to collect dust so choose what you keep up here wisely. If you store large serving dishes that don't fit into any of your cabinets, know that it is likely that you will have to wash them before you serve food on them.

If the sides of your fridge are a cacophony of artwork, colorful magnets, schedules, notes, and recipes, take everything off and start with a clean slate. Once everything is cleared from the vertical surfaces of your fridge, wipe down the sides, handle, and door ledges. While these surfaces are drying, decide what you really need or want to see on a daily basis.

A fridge covered in photos is a great conversation starter at parties. A beautiful magnet collection from all of your travels might also inspire stories and memories. Perhaps you'll designate an adult area for reminders and family schedules and a kid's area for artwork and photos. Personalize it for you and your family, but beware of too much clutter creeping back onto your fridge.

TIP 32

Clean Out the Refrigerator and Make a Shopping List

The refrigerator is where everyone goes multiple times a day and yet food still gets lost in there. For this 10-Minute Tidy, decide if you are going to focus on the shelves, drawers or doors. If you take everything off of the shelves, only put back what is still fresh. List whatever you may want to replace and be sure to wipe off the shelves while they are empty. I love keeping a magnetic note pad on the side of the fridge. This way everyone can write what he or she used up or would like to purchase.

The door of the refrigerator is usually where all the condiments end up. Condiments have a longer shelf life than produce but even mustard will grow mold if left in the fridge too long. Check all of your condiments for separation or discoloration. You may want to empty and recycle the almost-empty bottles and jars and start fresh. If you have condiments that no one likes, either serve it at your next party or just get rid of it. Condiments are a few dollars per bottle and can easily be replaced with a flavor that everyone loves.

The produce, dairy products and lunchmeats that end up in the drawers of your fridge are probably accessed the most frequently and are items that need to be stocked up on most often. Make a shopping list of what you need while you take inventory of what you already have.

If you don't clean out your refrigerator regularly, you may find some 'science projects' gone bad. Prevent this by taking inventory of your fridge every time you make a grocery list.

"My kitchen is a mystical place, a kind of temple for me. It is a place where the surfaces seem to have significance, where the sounds and odors carry meaning that transfers from the past and bridges to the future."
PEARL BAILEY

Sort Through Your Cookbooks

How many cookbooks do you have? How many cookbooks do you actually use? Do you have more cookbooks than time or inspiration? Don't be overwhelmed with too many options. Choose the cookbooks that you love, use, and enjoy referring to, and get rid of the rest.

Most homes have an all-in-one printer-copier-fax machine, so if you have some cookbooks that only have one or two favorite recipes in it, then photocopy those pages and donate the cookbook. Specialty cookbooks can be fun, but if the recipes take hours and are too complicated, then there is no reason to keep the cookbook, even if it was a gift. Someone else may love that really complicated Thai cookbook your friend gave you!

There are standard cookbooks to always keep as great references, such as *The Joy of Cooking*. The Internet is a great way to look up recipes anytime. Via the World Wide Web, you will find a million ways to cook chicken, rather than keeping 40 cookbooks that may repeat similar ways of preparing poultry. After sorting through all your cookbooks, donate unneccesary cookbooks and cooking magazines.

Create a Planned Menu for a Week or Month

Menu planning saves time and money for you and your entire family. Life is just easier when Tuesdays are taco night and Thursdays are burger night. There is still plenty of variety in this type of schedule because, for burger night you can serve hamburgers, turkey burgers, or garden burgers. By sticking to a general plan, you are not recreating the proverbial wheel every week and routines save time.

Some cookbooks are specifically written for weekly menu planning. By roasting a chicken on Monday, you can have chicken tacos on Tuesday and chicken salad sandwiches on Wednesday without any repetition or waste. The *Saving Dinner* cookbook and menu series by Leanne Ely, **www.savingdinner.com**, has gotten rave reviews from some of the moms I know.

Using a crock-pot, or slow cooker is a wonderful way to start dinner the night before and have it ready when you come home the next day. A crock-pot filled with a roast, carrots, potatoes and onions creates a hearty, well-balanced meal for your entire family in about 10 minutes or less!

Take the time to plan your menu for the week and it will save you extra trips to the grocery store for those last minute desperate dinner dashes. You can also menu plan for a month and have the grocery lists made up in advance to save even more time. Attaching coupons to the grocery list will save time and money too. Have fun doing your menu planning now so that you have more time to enjoy with your family each night.

Living Room

*"You can either take action
or you can hang back and hope for a miracle.
Miracles are great, but they are so unpredictable."*
PETER DRUCKER

The living room is often the first room that guests see when they enter your home. Therefore, this needs to be an area that is quick and easy to tidy. It's important to have a place for everything: books on the book shelf, magazines in the magazine holder, extra blankets and pillows either folded neatly in a corner or under one of the end tables.

Aesthetics are important in the living room, as this is also usually the main entertaining room. Group a collection of decorative items neatly, either hanging on the walls or on ledges and shelves. This allows the table surfaces to remain clean and clear of clutter.

Be sure that there is a home for everything, especially the items you use every day. Concealing all of the electronic equipment in an enclosed component will quickly clear the visual clutter. Perhaps your coffee table has a drawer where all of your remotes can be stored when not in use, or invest in a universal remote for simplicity.

If you have children, have a basket for each child's toys so that they can pick up their own toys at the end of each day. It is important that everyone in the house knows where his or her things should go so that everyone can tidy the living room in ten minutes or less! Ready? Set? Go!

"I am only one; but still I am one. I cannot do everything, but still I can do something; I will not refuse to do the something I can do."
HELEN KELLER

Recycle Magazines, Catalogs and Newspapers

An abundance of magazines, catalogs and newspapers can create stacks of clutter in your living room if they are not sorted and recycled regularly. Each month new magazines and catalogs arrive, whether you want them to or not! I have step-by-step instructions in **Tip 86** and **Appendix A** to remove your name and address from mailing lists. This is the quickest and easiest way to stop all the extra magazines and catalogs from being delivered to your home. You should also cancel any magazine subscriptions that you haven't read in the last two or three months because you can always buy an individual issue if you really want to read a particular article.

When a new magazine or catalog arrives, recycle the previous issue. You can also recycle both the current and previous issue if you know that you won't read either. Don't allow your reading material to pile up. If you do, the odds are likely that you will never catch up.

When you do read a magazine, tear out the pages you may want to reference again. Some magazines may have recipes, coupons, gift ideas, or websites you will want to use in the future. Be sure to sort all of your torn out pages into specific file categories and put them in the proper place. Recipes go in the kitchen, gift ideas go with the wrapping paper, and websites go near the computer.

I recommend getting rid of all the current weeks newspapers on Sunday when the new Sunday paper arrives. If you haven't read the paper by Sunday, then you certainly won't catch up once the work-week starts. Also, most newspapers and major articles can be read on the Internet so there's just no reason to keep old news!

TIP 36

Dust All Horizontal Surfaces in One Room

Most people don't enjoy dusting but with the right tools and only 10 minutes to maximize your efforts, you can dust an entire room. Grab your favorite dust rag or microfiber cloth and a stepstool and go to it! You can turn the music up while you're dusting just to make it more fun.

Set a timer for 10 minutes and start in one corner of the room and dust from the upper corner down. You may want to use a broom or extendable duster to reach to the ceiling in each corner to clear all the cobwebs. Use a chair or stepstool to dust off the tops of bookshelves, the entertainment center, and the ledges above the doors.

As you make your way around the room, be sure to dust all the bookshelves, tabletops, lampshades and the TV screen. As you pick up each individual item on each shelf, this is a good time to decide if you really want to keep this decorative piece. You may decide that you are tired of looking at it and you can put it in your bag of donations.

If you have a minute or two left during your 10-Minute Tidy, you can grab the Dustbuster and clean up the corners of the room as well as the baseboards along the wall. Heating vents are also areas that collect dust so vacuum those too.

"Real joy comes not from ease or riches or from the praise of men, but from doing something worthwhile."
PIERRE CONEILLE

One Plug Vacuuming

This is one of my most favorite ways to tidy in 10 minutes! Just plug your vacuum into an electrical outlet in a central part of your home and vacuum away. However far your vacuum cord reaches is how much you vacuum in each room. This is a great way to cover all of the main halls and passageways between rooms as well as being able to vacuum an entire room.

Give yourself permission to only go as far as the cord reaches. Of course, you can always extend your "one plug vacuuming" range by adding an extension cord! Have fun with this great idea my dear girlfriend Carla created.

If you want to extend this 10-Minute Tidy, get the vacuum attachments out and then the cleaning really begins! Vacuum the couch or chairs in your living room, under the beds, or along the baseboards and corners of a room. When was the last time that those areas were vacuumed?

Sort Book, Video and Music Collections

The living room is usually the main area where books, videos and music are located in the home. Your 10-Minute Tidy can focus on just one of these collections.

Books are one of the things that most people put on a shelf and rarely look at again. Now is the time to determine what you really want to keep. If you have a number of bookshelves, just pick one shelving unit and be sure to start at the top. If you start sorting books from the middle of the bookshelf, you will not be as efficient in completing this process. So, get a stepladder or stool if you need to, and read through the titles of the books starting on the left of the top shelf. Any books that you no longer want or need, pull them off and put them into a box.

While you are thinning out your book collection you may want to dust, add additional decorative items to the shelves, or stack some books horizontally to break up the visual monotony.

Unwanted books can be donated to a local library, school or children's center, depending on the subject of the book. If the books are valuable, you can either sell them online or to a local used bookstore. If you have a large collection of books you no longer want, consult a book dealer for a price on the entire collection.

VHS tapes, DVDs, and video games have an even shorter life span than books due to their diminishing entertainment value. These collections should be sorted through at least once a year as your family grows out of them or has seen them multiple times. This is also an opportunity to encourage your kids to trade games with their friends or resell their games to the video game store.

Music is more of a timeless collection that doesn't necessarily diminish in entertainment value, but I think we have all been occasionally disappointed in new music purchases. Unwanted CDs can be traded, sold or donated. Remember that each item should have a 'home', and by grouping your music alphabetically or by category, you will more quickly be able to decide on what you want to listen to.

Cassette tapes have become an outdated technology, like 8 tracks or 45 LP records. The universe grants you full permission to trash, donate or recycle your entire cassette tape collection if you have only been keeping them because you didn't know what to do with them!

Have Discreet Baskets
or Containers for Quick Pick-up

Grace has several baskets that are stored in cubbies in her living room for quick clean-ups at the end of the day or when guests are arriving. She has taught her children to each choose a basket that is easy for them to carry and put in the basket the things that belong in their rooms. This way, her children are empowered to take their basket into their room and put away their own toys, books and clothes.

Having extra, empty baskets that are stored discreetly hides what is in the baskets if you need to clean up in a hurry. As an added bonus, decorative baskets can serve as an attractive accent to your home!

If you don't have an area to store baskets in your living room, consider using plastic containers or collapsible laundry bins for quick storage solutions. Collapsible containers can be stored easily when not in use. It's always a good idea to have extra storage options on hand for quick pick-ups.

A Picture is Worth a Thousand Words

Photos are a wonderful way to capture the precious moments with your friends and family. Sometimes families have framed photos on every tabletop or bookshelf in the living room. This can be nice, but *hanging* your photos encourages you to clear horizontal surfaces and better use the vertical space in a room. Take 10 minutes to evaluate how the pictures are displayed in the living room. Is there anything that you would change?

In order to create visual harmony rather than clutter, choose one wall or shelf to display photos. A group of similar frames of different sizes will draw the eye to this area without it being the most prominent feature in the room. Hallways also make a wonderful gallery for photos to serve as a 'walk down memory lane'.

During this 10-Minute Tidy time, look at the pictures you have displayed objectively. If some of them are not as current, consider replacing the photos with newer ones and just reuse the frame. Pictures are wonderful snapshots of time and it is fun to have a variety of "captured moments" on display.

Water, Fertilize and Groom All Houseplants

This is a fun way to tidy because your plants will gratefully respond to your attention. Fill up your watering can, add fertilizer, grab the scissors and a trash bag and off you go!

Even though this is the Living Room chapter, start with the kitchen, since this is probably where most of your necessary tools are. Water, fertilize and groom all the plants in the kitchen. Be sure to cut off all the dead leaves and also notice which plants may need repotting. If any of your plants seem sick or infested with insects, take them outside or isolate them in a separate room so that you can treat them.

As you water and care for each plant, notice if it might do better being relocated. Does it need more sun or humidity? Perhaps there is a room in your home that doesn't have any plants. What would grow best in that room? Are there any plants that are just about dead or dying? If so, throw them out, or compost them, so that you are surrounded by living, thriving houseplants. I am amazed at how quickly some plants immediately perk up after being watered. This inspires me to go around my home each week and give each plant a few seconds of attention.

Bedrooms

"For each new morning with its light,
for rest and shelter of the night, for health and food,
for love and friends, for everything Thy goodness sends."
RALPH WALDO EMERSON

The bedroom is our place of rest and renewal. This sacred sanctuary is a beautiful space for sharing our most intimate moments. This is the very last place that we want any clutter. Bedrooms deserve special attention for tidying because they accommodate both the morning rush and evening relaxation. It's very important to keep this space clean and serene.

Enter your bedroom with 'new' eyes and look around…What clutter can be eliminated? How dusty or neglected does this space feel? Open up the windows and doors and have fresh breezes carry new energy into your bedroom. Once a season, strip off all the bedding and wash the dust ruffle, the mattress pad, the sheets, the duvet and the comforter. While everything is off the bed, flip the mattress over, too. This makes an amazing energetic difference!

You may want to wash or dry-clean the curtains, pillow shams and other decorative textiles you have in all of the bedrooms in your home. This is something you can have your kids help you with so that they learn to take pride in the cleaning of their bedroom as well.

I encourage you to spend a few moments tidying your bedroom everyday so that you can model made beds, clear floors, and spacious horizontal surfaces to your children. Ask them if they feel more relaxed in your bedroom or their own room. This can teach children to learn to read the energy of a room and realize the importance of having every bedroom as a sanctuary for rest and renewal.

Are you ready? Get set. Go tidy those bedrooms!

Strategies for Keeping Bedroom Floors Picked-Up

No one wants to be the 'Bad Cop,' but cluttered, littered bedroom floors aren't just messy, they're dangerous. No one wants to fall, trip or stumble during a midnight walk to the bathroom. Therefore, sometimes threats have to be made, even to the adults. A randomly kicked off slipper can be a stumbling block when your eyes are barely open. This has happened to me in the morning!

You could make the 10-Minute Tidy a nightly ritual for each member of your family. Have everyone pick up their rooms, as well as anything in all the common spaces throughout the house. Ten minutes of the same music at the same time each night would make sure that your home is tidied at least once every day as well as ensuring that there are no floor hazards lurking in the middle of the night.

Being a consistent role model by making your bed every morning and picking up the floors every night ensures both the safety and the support of everyone in the home. If everyone can keep their bedroom floors picked-up, there isn't any reason why the rest of the house can't be picked-up too!

TIP 43

Clean Off, Dust, and Organize Both Bedside Tables

It's amazing how much we stack on our bedside tables. Mine has lots of books in addition to the lamp and alarm clock. Now is the time to completely clear off the top of each bedside table and dust it. Evaluate everything as you put it back on your bedside table. Does it really belong there? If not, relocate the items that belong in the bathroom, living room or any other room.

Be realistic about how many books you can read at one time and only put back the books or magazines that you are currently reading. You have probably lost interest in a few of the ones that are only partially read. You can always get back to them later, but for now put them on a bookshelf in another room.

If your bedside tables have drawers, clean those out too. What do you really need to keep next to the bed? Remember that everything has energy and you only want to have pleasant memories or reminders next to you. This is a great place to keep a journal or a notebook to write down any brilliant ideas or dreams you have.

TIP 44
De-clutter the Top of Each Dresser

The tops of dressers are usually either tastefully decorated or a catch-all of everything. I tend to create little altars everywhere. I have a beautiful scarf or piece of fabric on top of each dresser and then I display my beautiful tchotchkes.

What is on the top of your dresser? Pretend that nothing is on top of it. What would you want on top of your dresser? Would you have just a few decorative pieces, or do you want to make room for a stereo or your jewelry collection? Visualize what you would really want there now. Once you have your ideal vision in mind, take off the items that you do not want there. Give away anything you no longer want to keep. After you have only the things you love on the dresser, take everything off, dust the top of the dresser and dust each item as you redecorate and put it back.

De-clutter the tops of the other dressers in your home one at a time. Be sure to ask for permission from the person whose dresser top you are clearing. Only organize what you have permission to make decisions about. If your children are young enough for you to make the decisions, display beautiful picture frames or other fragile items they are not able to handle by themselves yet. Rearranging the tops of the dressers will bring more beauty, order and calm energy to each bedroom.

Have fun knowing you can beautify each room in just 10 minutes at a time!

"Have patience with all things,
but chiefly have patience with yourself.
Do not lose courage in considering your own imperfections
but instantly set about remedying them
- every day begin the task anew."
SAINT FRANCIS DE SALES

Organize Two or More Dresser Drawers

Every bedroom usually has at least one dresser, some have even more! During your 10-Minute Tidy, choose two dresser drawers to sort and organize. Before you begin, have a bag for donations ready as well as a trash bin for those socks and underwear that just need to be thrown away.

Sort through each item in the drawer and decide if you want to keep it. Does it fit? Do you like it? How does this item make you feel? Everything from socks to t-shirts can be evaluated this way. Take each item out and either re-fold it neatly if you are going to keep it, or put it right into the donation or trash bag. Once the drawer is empty, wipe it out and then put back the neat stacks of clothes you want to keep.

You will be surprised when you have more room in each drawer because you can actually fit more clothes into a drawer when they are neatly folded, rather than just jumbled and jammed in. Be sure to leave extra room for whatever may be in the laundry that still needs to be put away.

Most dressers have a sock drawer. I recommend only keeping matching socks in the sock drawer. You can make your life easier by buying only the same brand and color of socks that each person in your family loves. That way, it's very easy to tell whose socks go in which dresser drawer.

Beware: The sock gnomes live in every home and occasionally hide a sock or two. I have never seen a sock gnome but I know that most of my clients have asked me where their single socks go. Where do missing socks go?!

I've created a system for the single sock dilemma. Have a container for all the single, un-matched socks in the house and once a month, when all the laundry is clean, sort the single sock basket. Any unmatched socks should be thrown out. The sock gnomes rarely return socks!

Label All Dresser Drawers

My friend Grace shared with me how labeling the dresser drawers in her home allowed anyone doing laundry to put things away correctly and more quickly. She has two children under four years old and her nannies help her with the laundry. Her mother also helps with the laundry when she's visiting. Now, with the implementation of the dresser drawer labeling systems, everyone knows where the clean laundry goes. As an extra bonus, her children get to learn how each article of clothing is spelled; the dresser drawer labels are words they learn to read.

If your children are very young, you can also have pictures of what goes in each dresser drawer so that they learn to pick out or put away their own clothes. These picture labels are also great for toys. When you write out the words under the pictures, they can begin to learn letters as well.

The labels on adult dresser drawers can be discreetly placed on the top ridge of the drawer. Choose a label that will stick to the wood but not remove the paint or finish. It really does feel great when you come home to the clean laundry already put away.

Iron Five Items

Ironing is not a chore that most people enjoy, but you can make a game out of it by seeing how many items you can iron in 10 minutes. I challenge you to iron five shirts in 10 minutes! If you don't iron five by the time the 10-Minute Tidy timer goes off, then perhaps you are motivated to keep going since you already have the iron hot and the ironing board set up.

Budget Closet™, Rev-a-Shelf™, and other closet organizing companies have compact ironing boards that pull right out of a standard size drawer. Look online to see a picture of how they easily unfold. You may want to consider having one of these compact ironing boards installed in your home. These are super convenient when you just need to touch something up quickly. You can also iron while watching television. I bet you can get a few pairs of pants ironed during commercials. Or, maybe you could watch a movie with your kids while ironing. This way you are all in the same room together but you don't necessarily need to be engaged with either the movie or the ironing, completely. Just be sure to keep your iron moving so that nothing gets burned.

Sort, Clean and Organize Your Jewelry

Jewelry is so beautiful and I keep mine in the bathroom because there is a huge mirror that I can use to determine which jewelry works with my hair and outfit that day. I also have jewelry that I don't wear very often, but still enjoy looking at. Now is the time to take 10 minutes to either 1) sort, 2) clean, or 3) organize your jewelry.

First, bring all of your jewelry to one area. The bed might be a larger surface for you to sort everything. This allows you to see that you actually have eight pairs of silver hoop earrings and you might be able to let go of a couple. You might notice that some silver is tarnishing.

A quick dunk in the jewelry cleaner and drying each individual piece with a polishing cloth will clean most jewelry.

Depending on the volume of each type of jewelry that you have, specific holders are designed for necklaces, earrings and bracelets.

Stacks and Stacks™, **www.stacksandstacks.com**, has a variety of jewelry organizers available online. They offer everything from travel containers, to watch cases for men, to wall organizers for large jewelry collections.

There are also drawer inserts made specifically for jewelry. Depending on the size of your drawer, you can build a great jewelry sorting system. Acrylic jewelry trays slide on the top of these drawer inserts. This almost doubles your storage capacity and everything remains easy to see.

You can create your own simple versions, too. For instance, hooks on the wall work fine for necklaces. Hanging your hook earrings on the side of a vase, container, or cup will allow you to keep your earrings in pairs and easy to see. Jewelry that is sorted and easily accessible is so much more fun to wear than untangling a mess when you're trying to get out the door in the morning or have a relaxing evening out. Enjoy your jewelry.

The 10-Minute
Room Rearranging Plan

It generally takes more than 10 minutes to re-arrange bedroom furniture, so this 10-Minute Tidy is just the visualizing and planning time. Bedrooms often get boring if the furniture is always kept in the same place for years. Every six months, reevaluate how each bedroom is arranged. Ask your children to be involved in the decision-making process for their rooms. If you are ready to change things around, you may want to measure furniture or sketch out the new floor plan.

Will the furniture be more balanced if certain heavy pieces, like the bed and dresser, are in different areas of the room? Can the dresser be relocated closer to the closet so that clothes are easier to access in the morning? Are certain pieces of furniture used infrequently and if so, could they be relocated elsewhere? For instance, you may want to add a desk in your child's bedroom, so the small table and chair set might need to be relocated.

When you are ready to move the furniture around, take the opportunity to find what's been "growing" underneath furniture: get rid of garbage, thoroughly vacuum the floors where the furniture was and dust the walls and baseboards.

Take ten minutes to look at each room with a fresh perspective and visualize how the room could be arranged differently. There are lots of possibilities!

"Try out your ideas by visualizing them in action."
DAVID SEABURY

Bedrooms

Have Quick and Easy Guest Bedding Ready

The more people in your home, the more likely you are to have overnight guests. My girlfriend Gwendolyn, with two teenagers, has devised a quick and easy solution for anyone staying over. She has already put together bedding sets for sleepovers that the kids can pull out themselves, and put away themselves.

You can use an old queen size feather bed folded in half that slides underneath a twin bed easily. Store the feather bed with a comforter already folded on top of it, plus a set of clean sheets and a pillowcase. The kids can set up the bed on their own, and then slide it back under the bed, putting the sheets by the washer in the morning. What a great, manageable idea!

For adult overnight guests, it's also important to have sheets, blankets and extra pillows all stored together for a quick and easy guest bed. You may want to store these items together in the linen closet so that you can grab them all in one armload. You could also store them in a clear, plastic comforter bag so that the guest can easily repack the blankets and pillow for next time. Having overnight guests is fun and having their bedding easily accessible makes their stay even more enjoyable.

Clear One Area of Your Child's Room: Toys, Books or Dolls

OK, I realize that 10 minutes is not a long time in your child's bedroom. Just pick one area to clear with them, whether it is the toy chest, the bookshelf or the doll corner. Sort through this one area and weed out any broken toys that need to be thrown out, books that are too basic for them now, or dolls that they no longer play with. Neat-Oh!™ has soft padded bins that easily box up dolls, toy animals, or car collections. Check out their creative containers for toys and artwork at **www.neat-oh.com**.

When sorting children's toys, be sure to respect their possessions and help them decide what to keep and what can be given to other children. Homeless shelters and women's centers are always seeking toys, books, dolls and clothes. Consider 'adopting' a shelter or center that you can consistently give all of your children's outgrown items to. You might even want to bring your children with you when you make these donations so that they can see all of the children who will benefit from their generosity. This could help make the process of weeding out their toys, books and dolls easier in the future.

Santa Cruz has a toy lending library for which you pay a small fee and then rotate the toys your children want to borrow for one month at a time. Allyson's son chose a microscope to take home for a month. She also donated several boxes of toys her son had grown bored of at the same time. What a massive win-win! Find out if there is a toy lending library in your town or nearby.

If you need containers for your child's toys, ask your child what they would prefer: clear or colored, plastic bins or baskets. Once you have the containers, have each child decide what they want to put into each container. When they put all of the cars in the blue box will they will kinesthetically reinforce their own organization system.

If you have a certain time of year, before their birthday or the holidays, that your children are expected to clean out their toys, it empowers them to make their own decisions. Give them a donation box, a 'sell' box and a garbage bag. Your children may want an opportunity to 'cash in' on their unwanted items. Consider allowing your children to sell whatever they don't want to a friend, online, or at a garage sale.

When organizing their books, toys, or dolls, use the bed as a sorting place so that you and your children have to finish sorting their stuff before bedtime. Organization is a great habit to instill in children at an early age. Generosity and sharing with others are also wonderful values to inspire in your children at every opportunity.

"One of the most important things we adults can do for young children is to model the kind of person we would like them to be."
CAROL B. HILLMAN

Bedrooms

Sort Puzzles and Games

Puzzles and games get their own time for sorting and evaluating. Some children love puzzles and some don't. Decide which puzzles you think your children may do on a rainy day and which may be too difficult or too easy for them.

Any puzzles that your children no longer want can be donated to a shelter or community center as long as all the pieces are in the box. Any boxes with missing pieces should be thrown away or recycled, as there is nothing more frustrating than doing a puzzle and having missing pieces at the very end. Think about the satisfaction of putting in the very last puzzle piece and admiring the completed work! Therefore, please only offer complete puzzles to others.

Family game nights playing board or card games can help children learn skills and strategies. Perhaps you'll come across a few games that might be fun for the whole family. Store those games in a place where you will see them, like the pantry or front hall closet.

If your well-loved game needs a new box, replacement boxes are available. A Monopoly™ game can have a snazzy new plastic box by Game Savers™, **www.obhenterprises.com**. I also recently saw these game boxes at the Container Store™. If the well-loved game has missing pieces, you can order replacement pieces online. Ehow™, **www.ehow.com** explains the process when you search 'replacement game pieces'.

Evaluate which puzzles and games your kids have mastered or those they are no longer interested in. Only keep the puzzles and games your family enjoys.

"Be aware of wonder.
Live a balanced life--learn some and think some
and draw and paint and sing and dance and play
and work every day some."
UNKNOWN

Create Files or Boxes
for Each Child's Memorabilia

Every child creates artwork masterpieces that must be kept forever—or so we think! I recommend that you create a portfolio file or box for each child's memorabilia. I also encourage you to make decisions about what to keep and what can be discreetly discarded. If you choose to have a file for each child, legal size folders are better since each art project might not fit neatly into an 8.5" x 11" folder. You may want to create a file for each year, age, or grade to organize and also limit the amount that you store.

If you choose to create a box for each child's memorabilia, then you have also created a "limited" container for their artwork and creations. Perhaps you can help your child decide what to store in their "Memory Box" by having them decorate the box inside and out with their favorite colors, pictures, or masterpieces. Teaching your child that they can't keep everything forever helps them learn basic decision-making and organizing principles at a young age.

As I defined in the introduction, "clutter" is just something that you, your child, or your spouse, hasn't made a decision about yet. Beginning to make decisions of what to get rid of, what can be given to others, what to keep, and where to keep it, empowers everyone to only keep the things they love. This type of organizational decision-making is an important skill throughout everyone's life.

"My overriding memory of childhood is having the freedom to decide which way to go in life and having my parents' support."
MICHAEL SCHUMACHER

Bedrooms

Download a Packing Checklist for Your Next Vacation or Camping Trip

It is important to be prepared when going on vacation or camping. Real Simple™ offers a packing checklist that you can easily download and then personalize to your family's specific needs at **www.realsimple.com/packingchecklists.** You can print, email or copy and paste this thorough 5-page list so that you have it as a reference every time you go away. This list will include most of what you will need to bring for adventures in sand, snow or safari! Real Simple™ is a fantastic resource for all kinds of organizing tips and solutions.

A packing checklist will save you time because you will be well prepared. A packing checklist also saves you money so that you don't have to buy replacement items you forgot at home. A great place to keep this packing list is in a Travel file. If you don't have a file for Travel, make one right now.

In your Travel file, keep information on your favorite places to go or that you want to explore in the future. You can have different sections in your Travel file for Local, United States, and International destinations. Be sure to keep your packing checklist right in front so it's easy to find every time you need it. You can also make multiple copies and add different items depending on if you are going camping or on a cruise.

Each member of your family can have a checklist depending on their individual needs. This teaches your children responsibility for their own belongings and prepares them for when they might travel on their own, whether to their grandparent's house or to camp. Lists are an important and easy way to save time and make your life easier!

Bathrooms

*"The achievement of your goal is assured
the moment you commit yourself to it."*
MACK R. DOUGLAS

Bathrooms get a lot of daily traffic. Isn't it amazing how often we use the bathroom and how rarely we pay attention to what is actually stored in there? Most families use the same 10-20 items and everything else is just stored here, there and everywhere. Have only what you need to use in the bathroom and get rid of the half empty products that are no longer used.

If your bathroom lacks storage, consider adding shelves on the walls, cabinets above or below the sink, or more drawers in the vanity. Target™ and **Organize.com** offer easy, inexpensive storage solutions. Get what you need to better organize the smallest room in your home.

Bathrooms must be functional, and it's really great when they are clean, organized and well decorated, too. One of the most common times a person looks under the sink is for an extra roll of toilet paper. What do your guests see when they look in your bathroom cabinets?

Once you have organized your bathroom, it's easy to maintain and keep clean. Are you ready? Get set. Go!

Organize a Bathroom Shelf

It's easy to keep the bathroom organized if you spend just 10 minutes at a time sorting the stuff in one area. Pick a small, specific area, like a shelf, and see how much you can clear off that you don't need or use. Most bathroom products have an expiration date on them so you can begin by checking those dates. If anything smells funny when you open it, throw it out. You don't want to put that in or on your body.

Any containers that can be recycled should be emptied and rinsed before they are recycled. Recycle as much as you can, from partial shampoo bottles to the paper boxes that toothpaste comes in.

Makeup should be thrown out if it has been open for more than six months. Mascara should be replaced after three months. There are great acrylic holders for different types of makeup. Only keep a realistic amount of lipstick that you will actually wear. Get a lipstick holder that keeps the tubes upright so that you can read the label on the bottom. Group lipsticks by color: reds, pinks, and corals so that your lipstick and outfit coordination is easy in the morning.

Store like-items together so that everyone can quickly find a particular product they are looking for. Keep lotions separate from shampoo or toothpaste. Only stock the products your family will use. Anything unwanted can be donated to a homeless shelter or women's center.

"If I want to be alone, some place I can write, I can read, I can pray, I can cry, I can do whatever I want —I go to the bathroom."
ALICIA KEYS

Clean Out the
Vanity Drawers

How does so much stuff end up in each drawer? Probably because most people just throw things in there without thinking. The top bathroom vanity drawers are the catch-all for everyone who uses that bathroom regularly. Consider having a designated drawer for each person.

Makeup will stay separate from shaving stuff if you designate what goes in each drawer. I also recommend using drawer organizers as often as possible so that different lotions and potions are separated based on their use. Space Savers™, **www.spacesavers.com**, has many different sizes and styles of drawer organizers depending on what your needs are. Whenever you order organizing containers, be sure to accurately measure the length, width, and depth of that area.

For a child's bathroom, use a plastic utensil holder for toothbrushes, toothpaste and floss. This plastic holder is easy to wipe out quickly or run through the dishwasher. Sort one drawer at a time and be sure to wipe out the bottom so that you are starting with a clean slate before putting anything back.

Sort and Organize
the Cabinets Below the Sink

Under the bathroom sink may be one of the last areas you want to spend time, but it will feel great to have sorted, purged, and organized this area once you are done! If you need inspiration, The Container Store™, **www.containerstore.com,** has a whole category for storage under the sink. Seeing what your options are might help motivate you to tackle this project.

Once your new under-the-sink storage solutions have arrived, you can get on the floor and get ready to clear out that area. Throw out anything that looks discolored or smells bad. Some lotions will have expiration dates. Sort out the things that you want to keep vs. the things that belong somewhere else vs. the trash. Group like-items together: soaps, lotions, sunscreen, and cleaning supplies. Get everything out, all the way to the back of the cabinet and then wipe out the empty cabinet.

Looking at this fresh, clean open space, decide what needs to be accessed the most often (toilet paper) vs. the least often (extra bath products). Put back only the products that your family will use. And, be sure to leave room for a basket of guest supplies. (See **Tip 58**).

TIP 58

Create a Guest
Supply Basket

What do you do with all those extra, travel size toiletries? As you go through each drawer, shelf and cabinet in your bathrooms, create one basket of supplies for your guests. This makes it very easy to put out the basket any time you have overnight guests. Store this basket under the sink or in a cabinet in your primary guest bathroom. A toothbrush and toothpaste are forgotten most often. Having a variety of new, individually packaged toothbrushes allows your guest to choose what type they prefer. A variety of trial size toothpastes are also fun to share.

My girlfriend with two teenagers has devised a toothbrush system for all their over-night guests. Here's Gwendolyn's system:

> *"I keep extra, new toothbrushes for guests (we have many who arrive without them, usually under the age of 13) and I've learned that permanent marker doesn't work well to mark on the actual toothbrush. I use a wide rubber band, like the ones that bind broccoli and asparagus, and we write their name on the rubber band. Then, they draw a symbol of their choice on the rubber band and wrap it around the handle*

with the symbol showing. I have a 'guest toothbrush' holder that is always full. It gives my kids and others' no excuse not to brush, plus it's fun for kids to find their toothbrush with the symbol they drew. Even 13 year olds get excited."

Thank you Gwendolyn for being such a great mom!

Scrub the Shower Doors
or Replace the Shower Curtain

Probably no one particularly likes scrubbing showers doors. I actually think it's easier to do while *in* the shower since I am already getting wet. If you only have 10 minutes to tidy, spray the cleaner on the shower doors and come back in five to seven minutes to wipe off the soap build-up. While the cleaner is working on the shower doors, you could clean the mirror, the sink and toilet. Finish with the shower doors.

If you can develop a habit of using a squeegee to wipe off excess water from the shower doors after each use, this will greatly reduce the amount of soap build-up.

If you do not have shower doors to scrub, evaluate your shower curtain. Does it need to be washed? Do you need a new liner? Would a new shower curtain really brighten up the bathroom? If so, buy what you need; it takes less than 10 minutes to hang up a new shower curtain or liner. What a difference!

Create an Organized
First Aid Supply Area

Most homes have lots of first aid supplies but rarely are they organized. It's important to have all the necessary supplies should an emergency occur, and being organized will help reduce the stress of any situation.

Begin by bringing all the household first aid supplies to one area. Decide where these are to be stored—probably the ground floor is best, either in the kitchen or bathroom. Next, determine what you are going to keep everything in; it should be portable, should an emergency occur outside or upstairs. A new fishing tackle box or handled basket would be a simple storage solution. Be sure whatever you choose fits where you want the first aid supplies to be stored. There are also great, ready-made first aid kits that have everything already in one container.

Once you have decided on the container, then you can organize your supplies. Group basics together: Band-Aids, peroxide, antibiotic ointment. Then have colds/flu medicines together with cough drops and the thermometer, perhaps, all in a clear, plastic bag. Next, have your emergency items: tape and gauze, ace bandages, pen and paper, and a first aid manual. You might want to also have a bee sting and/or snake bite kit depending on where you live. Be sure to check the expiration dates of your supplies and also make a list of anything else you may want to add to your first aid kit.

Show everyone in your home where the first aid supplies are stored. Give them a "tour" of what is in the box or basket and have general instructions so everyone knows what to do in case of an emergency. It is reassuring to have the first aid supplies stocked and well organized.

Closets

"Ability is what you're capable of doing.
Motivation determines what you do.
Attitude determines how well you do it."
LOU HOLTZ

Closets are areas of infinite possibility. Closets can be rearranged, re-configured or re-designated depending on what you need to use it for. My friend Lennie converted her deep kitchen closet into a small desk and workstation for her laptop. She has her home management projects all behind a closed door. Ingenious!

I love closets that are organized neatly and where everything is easy to find. Talya's walk-in clothes closet is filled to the brim with all her wonderful clothes and she even decorated the remaining wall space with beautiful art pieces that inspire her.

You can organize your closets in any way that suits your specific needs. The following tips are to help you weed out the things you no longer want or need and to develop the habit of only keeping the things you use or love. Have fun in your closets!

Ready? Set? Go!

Sort Through Your Hanging Clothes

I love organized clothes hanging on a rack. I have my clothes by category, color and style. By separating the pants from the tops, it's easy to assemble outfits depending on the weather and what you feel like expressing each day. If this arrangement appeals to you, read on for different ways to make it happen.

During this 10-Minute Tidy, just begin at one end of the hanging clothes bar and look at each item individually. Decide if it fits you and whether you love wearing it. If it doesn't fit right now, I highly recommend giving it away. Once you are at that particular size again, you deserve new clothes. If you just can't part with your old pair of jeans yet, consider putting them in a box. If you haven't gone into the box in three months, give everything in the box away because now you realize that you never really missed those clothes anyway.

If there are clothes that you don't like the color, feel or fit of, give those away too. You don't have to keep the Christmas sweater your grandmother gave you just to wear next Christmas. Give that sweater away; put it in your donation bag immediately. Only keep the beautiful clothes you love to wear.

Once you have gone all the way across the hanging clothes rack while pulling out items to give away or box up, begin sorting your clothes into categories. Some people like to group clothes together as prearranged outfits, which does save time when getting dressed. I also assure you that if you have all the pants in one area and all the tops in another area, you will create more interesting outfit combinations.

Consider grouping all the short-sleeve shirts together, separate from the long-sleeve blouses, so that it's easy to see what options you have depending on the weather. Hanging all the similar colored clothing together also helps you make faster outfit decisions on those mornings when you feel like you have "nothing to wear."

Having kids learn to organize their hanging clothes by separating school clothes from holiday or church clothes also helps them to dress themselves more quickly and appropriately in the morning.

Enjoy opening the closet doors and seeing neatly organized hanging clothes!

Select Five Articles of Clothing You Haven't Worn Recently

Let's face it: most of us have clothes that we haven't worn in a long time. In 10 minutes, you can try on at least five articles of clothing and decide whether you want to keep each one or give it away. I highly recommend that if you decide to keep something, even though you haven't worn it in a long time, that you put it closer to the front of your closet where you can easily see it. Being reminded of some of our lesser worn clothing can actually be a fun way to bring it back into wardrobe circulation.

This organizing technique is important to instill in your children as well. Having a bag where anyone can put his or her own clothes that no longer fit or that they don't want to wear anymore, saves time for both of you. Your children will only have clothes that fit them and that they like to choose from when they are dressing themselves. Then, you have less to put away or hang up for them.

Be sure to evaluate all the clothes that only get worn on special occasions. Do you really need to keep 12 suits when you no longer plan to go back to corporate work? Will four suits be enough for the next few years? Do you even need that many? Women's shelters would be very grateful to receive professional clothes since the women at the shelters are usually applying for jobs or just starting their careers over again.

What about ties? How many ties does one man actually need to choose from? Even though a tie will always 'fit,' it may not be in style, it could be stained, or is just plain ugly. Just be sure you have permission to sort and donate someone else's clothing!

No one needs to keep anything just because it was a gift. A gift is yours to keep and also yours to decide what you want to do with it. Give away anything that you no longer want to wear.

Keep a couple of the special occasion outfits for just that purpose: weddings, funerals, and holidays. A bridesmaid or prom dress that you won't ever wear again, ever, can be donated. I have worn some of those as costumes!

TIP 63
Rotate Your Seasonal Clothes

Depending on the climate you live in, rotating your clothes in the Spring and Fall adds more storage space and more variety to your everyday wardrobe. It is pretty unlikely that you need to have access to both shorts and wool sweaters at the same time. Decide what can be put away for a few months to allow more space for the clothes you want to wear right now.

Store your wool sweaters, turtlenecks, hats and gloves together for use when you need them again. Plastic storage bins with lids that snap shut prevent moths, moisture and rodents from getting in and eating your clothes. The dresser drawers that you used to store these items in are now empty and ready to be filled with shorts, bathing suits and tank tops.

You can actually use the same storage bins all year round and just rotate what is stored in them. I am always amazed when I pull something out and am excited to see it again. I will also sometimes pull out an item and decide that I am not interested in wearing it anymore. Those go into to the donation bag right away. If you don't love it or won't wear it, get rid of it!

TIP 64

Clear the Floor
of Your Bedroom Closet

Can you see the floor of your bedroom closet or is it piled with shoes, clothes, boxes and all sorts of random stuff? Don't feel guilty, you are not alone. Set your timer for 10 minutes and see how much dirty laundry you can pull out of the closet, how many clothes you can hang back up that fell down, and how many boxes can be relocated to other areas. Don't stop until you get to the bare floor.

The floor of the closet is a great storage place for whatever you decide suits your needs best. Be sure to clean the closet floor thoroughly before you put anything back. Your closet might need to have a laundry basket, shoe rack, and space for a few other boxes in it. The floor of my closet has my trunk of treasures on one side of it because I just couldn't bear the thought of having my most precious memorabilia stored anywhere else.

Your child may want to be able to play in his or her bedroom closet, so the floor would have to be kept clear. Another child might want to be able to get dressed on their own, so their closet might need a step stool for reaching the hanging clothes.

Depending on the size of your closet, you could also have

shelves or a small dresser in your closet for extra storage space. Every store that has home organization supplies will have a variety of storage solutions for your closet. Choose what will work best for each closet.

"The undertaking of a new action brings new strength."
EVENUS

Closets

TIP 65

Organize All the Shoes in One Closet

Shoes are necessary. Shoes can also be decorative, fun fashion for the feet. It's important to be able to find your shoes quickly and easily when you are getting dressed. Therefore, having your shoes organized will save you lots of time and reduce stress.

Pick a closet and see how quickly you can match up the shoes, deciding which ones you want to keep and which pairs can be donated. You may want to put together a shoe rack to create extra vertical storage space. Shoe racks can go on the floor of the closet, on the back of a door, or in compartments hanging from the hanging clothes bar. Whichever shoe organization method works best for your closet, only keep shoes that fit, are comfortable, and that you enjoy wearing.

Most people keep their shoes in the bedroom. I recommend keeping the filthy footwear closer to the outside door. Store muddy, wet, or sandy shoes in the garage or laundry room rather than in the closet with all your clean clothes. It is easier to maintain a clean house when everyone takes off their dirty shoes right where they enter the home.

If you have lots of shoes, separate the boots from the sandals and store whichever ones are currently out-of-season in either a different closet or further away from your everyday shoes.

Have fun organizing your shoes!

> *"If you ever feel like you're on the verge of a nervous breakdown, just follow these simple rules:*
> *First, calm down;*
> *Second, come over and wash my car;*
> *Third, shine all my shoes.*
> *There, isn't that better?"*
> JACK HANDEY (DEEP THOUGHTS)

Label the Shelves
in the Linen Closet

I had my very first organizing client when I was 12! My mom had me help her best friend who just had her second baby. Carol's linen closet was packed, and nothing was easy to find. I highly encourage you to sort your linens according to size, make neat stacks of sets, and then label the shelves. King sheets for the master bedroom need to be kept separate from the queen sheets for the guest room. Twin sheets for the kids' beds are in a separate stack from the crib sheets. If you label the shelves in the linen closet, everything can be quickly and easily put back in the proper location. When the sheets are stored as sets, it makes changing the bed linens even faster and easier.

This same system can be used for towels. Beach, bath and hand towels each need their own area in the linen closet. This helps you see at a quick glance how many of each category you actually have. The amount of space in your linen closet also limits the number of items that you can neatly store on each shelf. Remember, you can actually fit more things into an area when they are neatly folded.

TIP 67

Put Your Pictures in Photo Boxes

Organizing photos can take many hours—days even—if you haven't done anything with a lifetime of pictures. At the very least, storing photos in photo boxes protects them from dust and moisture. Photo boxes are also easily stacked and labeled on the front so that the photos can be quickly sorted into general categories or time periods until you can take the time to further divide them or put the photos into albums.

Purchase a few photo boxes and decide what is the best way for you to separate your photos. You could label the boxes by decade: 80's, 90's, and 2000's. This is a quick way to sort them in 10 minute increments. You could also sort by topic: Vacation, Family, and Holidays. Wouldn't it be fun to create a photo album containing 20 years of holidays?

Rather than store your photos everywhere (in closets, desk drawers, the kitchen), pick one place that all the photos will live. Have this location be able to accommodate the photo boxes, photo albums, and loose photos. I also recommend getting an album for your photo CDs so that these can be stored properly. Have fun sorting your photos and reliving the memories!

Tidy the Craft Area in Your Home

Every house has some type of craft area. Even though I don't have kids, I still like to have pastels, colored pens and pencils, and paints around for those moments of creative expression. If you have kids, I'm sure that your craft supplies are multiplied exponentially.

Separate baskets or containers for pens, pencils, paints, paper, glue, glitter, stickers and various other materials, allows for easy set-up and clean-up. Plastic tablecloths or shower curtains on both the table and the floor under the table allow anyone to unleash their full creativity and still have easy clean-up.

It's important to also instill responsibility for cleaning up those creative 'messes.' A clean-up song and dance will help the clean-up process go more smoothly, and some kids even like to take out the trash or use the Dustbuster to vacuum up all the tiny bits scattered on the floor.

Crafts are fun and it's important to have the materials separated into the different types of projects (knitting, clay, painting). Organization saves time and makes it more fun to express yourself creatively.

Office

"You can only improve the results of a recurring system.
You cannot improve the results of a one-time only effort."
UNKNOWN

Every home needs an office. It doesn't have to be an entire room devoted to a desk and computer. Some kitchens have a built-in office area that works great as the household 'command center.' Even choosing a table as a dedicated office area will work.

One definition of an office is "an area where actions and activities are accomplished." Your home office area may be devoted to bill paying, whereas someone else may pay all of his or her bills online at work. Another home office might be the family command center where the phone, calendar, and bulletin board are located to manage the schedules of everyone in the house. Even having your basic office supplies all in one area allows you easy access to everything you would need to pay a bill, check your schedule, or write a card.

Have your office be a place where you can be productive and get things done. If your office is chaotic and cluttered, what type of concentration and productivity are possible in there?

Now is the time to organize your office. Ready? Get set. Go!

Relocate the Trashcan, Recycling Bin, and Shredder So that All are Within Reach

This 10-Minute Tidy Tip ensures you more ease for dealing with all the various papers that enter your home. Taking a few minutes to relocate a trashcan, recycling bin and shredder closer to your desk allows you to quickly get rid of any papers that you do not want to keep. Deciding what to do with the papers you want to keep is in the next chapter (**Papers**).

If you don't feel like there is room for the trashcan, recycling bin and shredder to all be within arms reach of where you sit at your desk, ask yourself, what can be moved or relocated so that this is possible?

Every home should have a shredder to protect your identity. If you don't have one, your local office supply store usually has many to choose from. Buy a shredder that cuts papers into bits, not strips. Strip cut shredders are no longer sufficient. If you own a strip-cut shredder, now is the time to upgrade your shredder to a confetti-cut shredder. Most new shredders also allow you to shred credit cards and CDs. Buy the best shredder that you can afford because the cheaper it is, the shorter its lifespan, and you'll want a shredder that works well every time you use it, for a long time.

Be sure to oil your shredder occasionally with shredder oil or lubrication sheets, available at office supply stores. It is also important to turn off or unplug your shredder if you have dogs or small children in your home as shredders can be dangerous if not used for their proper intent.

Sort Office Supplies in Your Desk Drawers

Set your timer for 10 minutes and start with the desk drawer you use the most. See what you can do to organize this one drawer. If you have more time or enthusiasm, continue to organize each drawer in your desk. You just might be amazed at what you find in there.

There are desk drawer organizing trays that are perfect for sorting all your various supplies. Office Max™, Office Depot™ and Staples™ all have office organizing supplies that you can purchase online or at your local store. It's important to have the things you need on hand but beware of excess. Do not order office supplies that come in huge quantities that you won't ever use in a lifetime!

Keep basic supplies right on top of your desk so that pens, pencils, scissors and notepaper are easy to grab and use. Use a tray organizer to corral and limit the quantity of supplies you keep in your desk drawers. Plastic drawer trays easily separate writing utensils from paperclips and pushpins. These trays are usually stored on the bottom of the drawer but can also slide along the top of the drawer to create more storage room below the tray.

If your office supplies are scattered throughout your home, gather them all right now and designate one place where all office supplies will be kept. Each person in your home may have different project needs so get the right supplies for each project, but be sure to keep your desk drawers uncluttered. If you can't find what you are looking for in 10 seconds or less, then you probably have too much in there, and it's time to sort your desk drawers.

Organize the Office Supply Cabinet

I love office supplies. I was one of those kids that when my mom took me to the grocery store, the office supply aisle was my favorite place to go. Were you like this too?

Office supplies are fun because they allow you great options for those creative moments. And they satisfy a need to be prepared as well. Therefore, having an organized, well-stocked office supply cabinet is important.

How much you can actually store depends on where you keep the extra office supplies that don't fit in your desk. Remember that organized areas actually allow you to have more stuff in them, but the key is to be able to see and grab whatever you need quickly and easily. You do not want to set items in front of each other if they are blocking the view of rear items, and it is important to store things so that you can read what is in each box or bag.

Store similar items together such as paper, labels, writing utensils, filing supplies, etc. The larger containers and boxes that these items come packaged in are properly labeled and usually easy to see, so keep supplies in their original packaging.

Keep only what you will use and donate anything that you have too much of or will no longer use. Shelters and children's clubs are always thrilled to receive office supplies. School teachers also have limited funding for their classroom supplies; I highly encourage you to donate any surplus office supplies you have.

> *"Teacher appreciation makes the world of education go around."*
> HELEN PETERS

TIP *72*

Donate All Old or Excess Office Equipment

You are not alone if you have old office equipment in your home that you don't know what to do with. Where do you take old computers, fax machines, telephones and all those extra cords and gizmos? You're not sure if they can be recycled, but you know that it's not good, or maybe even allowed, to just throw them in the garbage, so where should they go?

Unused electronics can be recycled and sometimes even refurbished and given to others. Some schools, shelters, and churches will accept electronics that are still in working order. Be sure to donate all the proper cords and any extra ink, paper, or toner that you may have for that machine.

There are also businesses that will accept particular electronics. Most cell phone companies have a donation program: if you take your old cell phones to them, they will remove the previous information and donate the phones to those in need.

The Environmental Protection Agency (EPA) is a government agency that lists many resources for donating, recycling, or trading in your electronics. They have a specific listing for each of the major computer manufacturers if you want to send back your old equipment. The information is located at: **www.epa.gov/epaoswer/hazwaste/recycle/ecycling/ donate.htm#mftr.**

E-waste is electronic waste and companies collect electronics that may or may not be working. Look online under "electronics recycling" for an e-waste collection service near you. You will be amazed at all of your options. Old or excess office equipment is just cluttering your space. Do the right thing by getting rid of it properly.

Delete Unwanted Files
From Your Desktop

How cluttered is your computer desktop? Can you see the beautiful scenery you chose for your computer screen background or is it covered in file icons? I bet that you can clean up your desktop in 10 minutes or less!

Storing documents on your desktop is usually not a conscious decision; they just end up there when you download something. It's important that you decide what you really want on your desktop and what can be stored for easy access later. You are not working on all of these documents at the same time anyway so streamline your focus by putting the other documents that have been sitting on your desktop into the proper files for later use.

This same principle applies to shortcut icons. Evaluate what you use everyday and anything else should be eliminated. Do you really need 27 application shortcuts when seven will do? If you only use a shortcut icon occasionally, it only takes a few more seconds to access the program through the Start menu.

Eliminate clutter from all areas of your life, even the electronic spaces.

Run a Back-Up on Your Computer

Do you back-up your computer regularly? If not, take the next 10 minutes to run a back-up and save your recent documents to another location: CD, zip drive, memory stick, or network server, etc. Regular backs-ups will save you time and greatly reduce your stress if you lose any document and have to recreate it, or heaven forbid, your computer gets a virus, or your disk crashes.

The more people who access and use one computer, the greater the risk of user error. Meaning, if your kids use the same computer you use for your finances, be sure to back-up regularly. Back-ups also help you maintain and protect data on your computer. Data files and software files are saved during a back-up as an emergency copy.

Did you know that your hard drive degrades over time? I didn't. It's also susceptible to crashing. If you have a back-up copy of your data, you will not have to recreate all of it. Computers, software and people are not perfect so it's important to keep vital files saved in other locations. Take the time right now to run a back-up on your computer. This could take more than

10 minutes initially, but it's time well spent and an investment in your future sanity.

> "The great thing about a computer notebook is that no matter how much you stuff into it, it doesn't get bigger or heavier."
> BILL GATES

Office

Delete Unnecessary Email and Unsubscribe From Mailing Lists

Have you heard about the great book, *The 4-Hour Workweek*, by Timothy Ferriss? He recommends not even checking your email before 11am! Could you do that? It's a great goal to work towards.

Here is a list of ways that you might want to implement to reduce the daily clutter and distraction of emails:

1) Turn off the alert sound that goes off every time a new email arrives.

2) Turn off your pop-up windows.

3) Check email only when it is on your schedule to do.

4) Deal with "to do" messages that can be forwarded to others immediately, and move the more time-involved messages to your "Task" list and work them into your daily schedule.

5) When your name is in the cc section, you are not to respond unless your input is critical, or unless the person being addressed is not available.

6) Create new subject lines as the subject changes.

7) All subject lines should be as descriptive as possible so the person receiving it can determine in advance if they should open and deal with it then, or wait until they have more time.

8) All matters that need immediate or urgent attention are not to be handled using email. If it's important and time is an issue, pick up the telephone.

What do you find to be most effective in removing your email clutter?

"All great achievements require time."
DAVID SCHWARTZ

Office

Create Folders in Your Email Accounts

In the chapter on organizing the papers in your life, **Tip 89**, it suggests that you label your electronic files and folders the same as your paper files. It is also important that you create folders in your email accounts that have the same names as your electronic and paper files. Therefore, your Action files should be replicated in your email account: Call, Research, Delegate. Once you have taken the action that is required for that particular email, then you can move the message out of your Action folder and into your email Reference folders by topic: Specific Project, Certain Person, Particular Group.

Creating folders for the various electronic newsletters you receive is also important if they serve as reference materials you will go back and read again. I caution you to consider what you really need to save. When it comes to email, most people save too many messages, never to go back to them again. Remember that most of the time, you can either email and ask the person for that information again or look it up on the Internet.

Folders in your email accounts will save you lots of time when trying to find a specific message or topic again.

TIP *77*

Delete Old Contacts From Your Cell Phone

Have you ever deleted anyone from your cell phone contact list? Now is the time to scroll through your list of contacts and decide if you really need to keep all 500 of those phone numbers!

Start with the top of the list and look at each name and determine whether you still talk to that person regularly. If you can't even remember whom the name belongs to, look at the phone number to see if that prompts your recall. If you don't recognize the name or the phone number, consider deleting that contact from your cell phone. You are not going to call someone you don't remember, and if they call you, you can get their number again.

This is something you can do while waiting to get your oil changed, while at the airport, or any time that you are idly waiting somewhere. This process also reminds me to call clients I haven't heard from in a while, as well as old friends I want to reconnect with. What a great way to clear clutter and stay connected at the same time!

Register All Your Phone Numbers on the Do Not Call List

To stop annoying sales calls during dinner, call **888-382-1222** from your home phone to be put on the National Do Not Call list. You can also register your phone numbers online at **www. donotcall.gov.** This blocks your phone numbers for five years! You can register up to five numbers, so be sure to include all of the cell phone and land line numbers that your family uses.

Registering on the National Do Not Call list is an important way to stop intrusive phone solicitations from disrupting your time. Be sure to tell your friends, family and colleagues about this important registry to preserve your privacy.

Photocopy All the Important Items in Your Wallet

Take 10 minutes to photocopy all of the important items in your wallet right now. This might be one of the most important stress-reducing things you can do for yourself. Be sure to photocopy the back and front of your driver's license, credit cards and other identifying information. Keep the photocopies somewhere locked and safe in your home or office. This is also easy to do if you have a scanner and can scan the images into your computer.

Hopefully your wallet is never stolen or lost, but if it is, you will now have all of the important phone and account numbers you need in order to have the accounts closed or your cards replaced.

This is also a great opportunity for you to clean out any old pieces of paper you no longer need to be carrying around, and be sure to shred anything that has your signature, account number or any other identifying information on it.

Feel great about taking 10 minutes to protect yourself as well as clean out your wallet!

TIP 80

Photocopy All Documents in Your Safe-Deposit or Fire-Proof Box

If you have a safe-deposit box, hopefully you have already photocopied and/or scanned everything that is in there. Fireproof boxes are also becoming more common in homes. These portable safes protect your most important documents from being destroyed by fire, earthquake, flood or other natural disasters. Because of their portability, they are not as secure as a mounted safe is in your home.

Originals of the following should be stored in a safe-deposit or fire-proof box:

- Birth certificates
- Passports
- Property titles
- Property deeds
- Vehicle titles

- Social security cards
- Insurance policies
- Bonds and stock certificates
- Wills and Trusts
- Marriage, business and professional licenses

You may also have other important documents that require extra protection. Be sure to photocopy every page of each document and store the copies in another area outside of your home—perhaps out of state, at a relative's home. Then you could reciprocate keeping important documents for them.

Consider which documents will also need to be kept with your lawyer or executor. Creating a list of all of your financial accounts with account numbers and who to contact in case of an emergency is also an important document to store safely, perhaps password protected on your computer.

Make a comprehensive list of what is in your safe-deposit or fireproof box and keep it in a locked place. Keep one key to the safe deposit or fire-proof box in a safe place in your home and mail a second key to a friend or relative out of town, perhaps even out of state, just in case a natural disaster strikes. By taking a few moments now to copy and store your most important documents properly, you will save you and your family many hours of stress and frustration later.

TIP 81

Order Prints From Your Digital Camera

Most of the time we download pictures from our digital cameras so that we can look at them and share the photos with others electronically. But, printed photos, like a hand-written letter sent via snail-mail…well, there's something extra special about them.

If you haven't ordered prints in a long time, take 10 minutes right now to print photos at home or sign up with a printing service online. Kodakgallery™, Shutterfly™ and Snapfish™ are some of the frequently used sites for digital prints. Your local photo labs will also print photos from your digital camera.

If there is a special event or holiday coming up, now is a great time to order prints. Printed photos make great gifts for friends and family and can be easily sent with thank you and birthday cards. Enjoy sharing your photos with others.

Send Handwritten Cards

Don't you love receiving handwritten cards? Most of us don't write cards very often anymore. Emailing cards has replaced the traditional Hallmark card. I really feel a deeper connection with the person who sends me a handwritten card.

In 10 minutes you can actually write several cards if you already have cards on hand. Most desks that I have organized have cards in stock to send out. Mary actually has two file boxes of cards sorted by category, as well as three drawers of other cards that aren't sorted. I bet it is wonderful to receive a card from her! You don't need that many options to find an appropriate card to send to someone you care about, but being prepared for any occasion without making a trip to the store does save time.

Take the time right now to write a thank you card, a birthday card, or send someone you cherish a love note. It really does feel good!

TIP 83

Order Presents Online

Ordering presents online makes life so much easier than dealing with stores, parking and crowds. **www.Gifts.com** has a variety of gifts to choose from as well as the option to use their calendar system to remind you when important dates are approaching.

You can also utilize your computer, cell phone, or PDA calendar to keep track of special occasions. Set up each date with a reminder a week or two in advance so that you can order a gift and have it delivered on time.

Did you know that some websites actually keep track of when you order gifts, and will send you emails inquiring if you would like to order that item again? ProFlowers™ will remind you when the anniversary of the last time that you ordered flowers is approaching. This helps you get that bouquet of flowers to Mom on her birthday!

Order presents online today or enter a few dates into your calendar that will give you a reminder when the next special occasion is approaching. This may take less than 10 minutes but will be so very much appreciated by all of your friends and family.

Papers

"You must take action now that will move you towards your goals. Develop a sense of urgency in your life."
LES BROWN

Have you ever felt like you were drowning in paperwork? Papers can be the bane of many peoples existence. Everyone receives lots of paper everyday and most people can't keep up with their daily inflow. The key to paper management is to create places to store the papers that you need or want to keep. This chapter provides quick and simple strategies to manage your papers more easily and efficiently.

It is important to eliminate the papers that you do not need before they become pieces of the piles. Get off mailing lists; don't accept extra subscriptions just because the neighborhood kids are having a fundraiser; refrain from printing out anything that can be easily looked up on the computer or at the library later.

Most households receive approximately 41 pounds of junk mail each year! **Appendix A** gives you easy, step-by-step instructions on how to rid yourself of junk mail. Recycle as much as you can and encourage others to do the same. Ready? Set? Go!

Sort Today's Mail

Are you one of those folks who can't wait for the mail to arrive each day? Or, do you begrudgingly collect your mail and simply add it to the pile of yesterday's mail? If you're the latter, then consider the following practice.

Start by sorting today's mail. Then sort yesterday's mail. Then sort last week's mail until all the mail has been sorted. Some clients have boxes of unopened mail and it actually gets easier the older the mail is because most of it can be recycled or shredded immediately.

To sort today's mail, begin by separating the junk from the interesting stuff. Most of it is junk that can be recycled or shredded right away. Create categories for the things you want to read, the bills to pay, and the catalogs and flyers that you want to glance at. See **Appendix A** to learn more about removing your address from junk mailing lists so that you can stop receiving all of those credit card and mortgage offers.

I sort my mail on the walk from the mailbox to the kitchen. Using my fingers as dividers, I separate the junk from the bills from the other items. By the time I get to the kitchen, I can easily recycle the junk, leave the catalogs and flyers on the kitchen counter to look at later, and take the bills to the office to be paid.

The more that you can eliminate quickly, the easier it is to manage. Don't open mail and then put it back in the envelope. Decide now! Only keep what you need and recycle the extra inserts and envelopes. This process gets easier each time you do it. You, too, will be able to sort the mail on the walk from the mailbox into your home!

"What the world really needs is more love and less paperwork."
PEARL BAILEY

Set Up an Easy Mail Processing Area

If you receive a large volume of mail every day and you can't sort it on your way back from the mailbox to the kitchen or office, you may want to set up a mail processing area. Pick a place where you have a clear surface area and are also within reach of the trash, recycling, and shredder. This could be in your office or kitchen.

Chris sorts her mail in the laundry room after dinner. With a glass of wine to keep her company, she looks at each piece of mail and decides what to do with it. Her laundry room has a trashcan, recycling bin, and cubbies for each household member. She also has a basket for catalogs. She stacks the magazines that will go on the coffee table. She opens the bills and makes a pile of them to take into the office.

You can create this type of scenario, too, in which sorting the mail becomes an easy process. I recommend first selecting a place where it's convenient to have all the important pieces you will need every day in the same place. You can also make this area fun by adding a beautiful letter opener, decorative recycling bin or magazine basket, and perhaps put up inspiring photos or images so that you are looking at ideal travel destinations rather than wallowing in the bills. A mail processing area will make this an easier process so that you can keep up with the mail every day.

> *"When you make an efficient choice in moments of indecision, you establish more effectiveness within a given time span, saving energy and stress."*
> DOC CHILDRE

TIP 86

Remove Your Family From All Junk Mail Lists

There are three easy options for removing the name of everyone in your household from junk mailing lists:

1. Online: **www.stopjunk.com** or **www.dmaconsumers.org**
2. Call: National Opt-Out Center: **1-888-567-8688**
3. Write: Direct Marketing Association
                Mail Preference Service
                PO Box 282
                Carmel, NY 10512

They also offer an online form at **www.dmaconsumers.org/mailform.php** that you can print out and mail in.

Your sample letter should state: "I want to reduce the amount of unsolicited mail I receive. Please remove my name and address from your mailing list." Include all variations of your name: Bob Smith, Robert Smith, B. Smith, etc. with your Name, Address, City, State, Zip, and Signature.

This is well worth your time!

Sort Your Inbox

Wherever you sort your mail, you probably also have an Inbox or basket where the "Things To Deal With" live. Those plastic, often stacking 3-sided bins are the most common Inboxes and the ones I highly *discourage* you from using.

I suggest that you change your Inbox from one horizontal pile into a few vertical file folders. It is much easier to find the bills to pay when they are all together. It is also easier to find the time-sensitive documents when they are separated from all the other miscellaneous mail that you have decided to keep. For instance, you know that there is an invitation in the Inbox pile somewhere, but how quickly can you find it?

The goal is to eventually replace the Inbox with vertical Action Files. Create files depending on the action that needs to happen. Bills to Pay, Events to Schedule, Things to Read, and whatever other particular projects that need your attention are good Action Files to make. These Action Files live in the area where your horizontal Inbox was.

This way, you sort through every piece of paper in your Inbox and decide what the next action step is with each one. I recommend using file pockets instead of file folders. File pockets have sides on them; so if you have a "Calls to Make" action file, this is where business cards or Post-its go until the calls are made.

A tiered file pocket holder is a great way for you to have all your action files in one area. It will take up either the same or less space than your Inbox and you can clearly see each labeled file pocket. Follow this link to see an example of a tiered file holder: **http://www.organize-everything.com/stepsorter.html**.

I also recommend keeping your Action Files within arm's reach of where you sort your mail, your computer, and the trash and recycling bins. This way you can look at each piece of paper and take the next action step needed without having to get up and go somewhere else.

To keep things in perspective, remember the wise words of Richard Carlson, author of *Don't Sweat the Small Stuff.* Remind yourself that when you die, your "In Basket" won't be empty. So, if your kids are begging you to spend time with them or your spouse wants to go out on a date, stop sorting your Inbox, and enjoy sharing time with the ones you love.

File the Piles Stacked on Top of the Filing Cabinet

Do you have piles waiting to be filed? You are not alone. Now is the time to file all of the papers that you have stacked on top of the filing cabinet.

Begin with each piece of paper and decide where the best place is for you to find it again. Has a file already been created? If so, great! Slide the most recent papers in the front of the file folder. If there is not a file folder for the document you are holding, create a file with a general enough label so that this will not be the only piece of paper ever to be stored in this file.

See how many papers you can file in 10 minutes. The more thorough the filing system you have, the easier your filing will be. Your goal right now is to get to the bottom of the pile that's waiting to be filed.

Your future goal is to not accumulate papers that will simply sit and wait to be filed. Otherwise, how can you find any of the papers you want to keep unless you sort through those "To Be Filed" stacks? Once you have decided that you want to keep a paper, decide where you want to keep it and either file it or make a file for it immediately. It is important to have a supply of file folders, hanging files and plastic tabs on hand.

Brother™, **www.brother-usa.com/ptouch/**, has created P-touch label makers that are affordable, reliable, and easy to use. This is an excellent resource for making legible labels for all areas of your home and office. These label makers allow you to change the font size so that you can label everything from keys to storage containers. Printed filing labels also look more professional and you don't even need to use the computer. I love my label maker and I hope that you get one too!

Organize and Label Electronic Files to Match Paper Files

I know this chapter is about paper, but I also want you to know that your life will be easier if your electronic files follow the same organizational structure as your filing cabinets. If you just finished organizing your filing cabinets, open up your electronic files or "folders" and look at what files are called in both the electronic and paper versions. Are they the same, or different? Which label is more appropriate or easier for you to remember?

Rename your files or folders so that both the electronic and paper files match. It doesn't matter which file name you choose as long as it makes the most sense to you (unless you share files with others).

Do this for 10 minutes at a time and see how many identical labels match between the electronic and paper files. This process can go twice as fast if you have someone else read one set of file names and you read the other. Go slow enough to ensure accuracy and take the time to change the label if you need to. This process will ensure an accurate and compatible filing system for you and your documents.

Remove, Shred or Archive Old Files

Most filing cabinets either don't get used or never get cleaned out once they are filled. In 10 minutes, you can sort through quite a few files in one drawer of your filing cabinet. Begin with the very front of the drawer and decide if you still need to keep that first file folder. If you don't need to keep that file anymore, can the contents be recycled or do they need to be shredded?

Recycle the entire folder rather than reusing it if the file folder is old and tattered. Shred the file contents immediately if you no longer need to keep that information. See how many files you can clean out in 10 minutes. If you know that you will have a lot of papers to shred, consider putting them all in a bag or box and having a professional document shredding company pick up and process the entire box for you.

If you are inspired to keep going, work as long as you can to remove the files you no longer need to keep, and thin out the files that you do want to keep by seeing if what's inside of each folder can now be recycled or shredded. When you need to stop, place a bright colored Post-it sticking up as a place marker for you to know where to resume your removing, shredding, or archiving file process.

Papers

Keep sorting through your file cabinets until you have gone through each file. Each file drawer should be gone through and evaluated at least once a year. This may need to be done more often if your file cabinets tend to fill up more frequently. January is the best time to purge old files, collect the files needed for taxes, and to create files for the new year.

Most tax-related documents need to be kept for seven years. You can archive these documents in plastic file boxes with tightly sealed lids. Store these archived file boxes either in the closet in your office or the garage or attic of your home. It is unlikely that you will need them, but they are very important to have in case of an audit. **Appendix B** lists the most important items to keep and how long to store them. Consult with your tax advisor if you have specific questions.

Shred or Relocate
Archive Files

You may want to create more space in your file cabinets. Keep particular files or documents for long-term storage as archives. Move archive information to another area, such as the garage or a storage closet. You can also scan documents into your computer (or onto a CD) if the paper versions are not as convenient to keep.

Archive files stored in plastic file boxes will greatly reduce the likelihood of damage from insects, rodents or moisture. Plastic file boxes have lids that snap shut so that nothing can get in. These boxes are also easy to stack and label so that you can readily identify what is inside without having to take them out of the stack.

Read **Appendix B** to determine what you need to keep, how long you need to keep particular documents, and what can be recycled or shredded. Be sure to shred anything with your signature, social security number, or account number on it.

If you have a volume of papers to shred, don't burn out the motor of your home office shredder. Shredding companies can process spiral and 3-ring notebooks, photos, slides, CDs, bound reports, and much more.

Check the yellow pages for a local shredding service and arrange for them to come to your home or office to pick up your boxes of items to be shredded. Be sure to ask if the shredding company is licensed and bonded to prevent identity theft. Shredding companies are a great service that will protect your identity and put your mind at ease.

> *"If in our daily life we can smile,*
> *if we can be peaceful and happy,*
> *not only we, but everyone will profit from it.*
> *This is the most basic kind of peace work."*
> THICH NHAT HANH

Finances

*"The greatest danger is not that our aim is too high and we miss
it but that our aim is too low and we reach it."*
MICHELANGELO

Money flows through our lives just like water, sometimes
plentiful, sometimes just a trickle. It is important to manage
your finances properly and I have offered seven ways for you to
maintain your finances more easily.

What do you do with all of your financial papers? Are they
stacked somewhere or strewn about? Do you keep everything,
even though you never open the envelopes? You will learn
simple solutions for dealing with these papers, statements, and
receipts.

Internet banking and financial software programs empower you
to more easily manage your money. Signing up for automatic
bill paying allows you the peace of mind to know that you will
never pay a late fee again! Setting up an automatic savings plan
or tithe is also easy to do online.

With the number of credit card offers most people get in the
mail, there is no reason to pay interest on your credit card
balances. The savings of 0% interest is a reward in itself. I

encourage you to move your credit card balances to new cards with 0% interest, or the lowest interest rate you qualify for.

Are you ready to have your money flowing to you and through you more easily? Are you ready to keep and grow more money than you have ever had before? It can be done in 10-minute increments! Ready? Set? Go!

> *"Don't wish for it.*
> *Work for it."*
> UNKNOWN

Create an Easy Receipt
Storage System

Do you keep receipts? Why do you keep them? Where are they stored? **Appendix B** gives you an idea of what receipts to keep and for how long.

If you need to keep receipts, it's important to create an easy system to store them. I recommend a 13-pocket, half-size, accordion file folder, called a "check file". These can be purchased at most office supply stores for less than $5 and are typically plastic or heavy card stock. Each of the 13 pockets can be labeled according to your receipt categories.

You may need just broad categories such as Restaurant, Clothing, Gifts, Donations, and Electronics. If you do not have a home-based business, you really only need to keep receipts for items you may want to return or for 'large purchase price' items. Most people cannot deduct their gas or groceries, so these receipts can be readily recycled. Shred all receipts with your signature or full account number on them.

If you have a business (home-based or otherwise), Advertising, Auto, Gas, Postage, Meals, Office Supplies, Phone, Training,

Travel, and Utilities are some examples of how to categorize your receipts. You may want to create specific categories based on your particular business. Look at how your tax return line items are delineated for other receipt categories.

Once you decide on your categories, it's easy to label each section and quickly sort your receipts. Keep your receipt storage system in a place where you would empty out your wallet. That way it's easy to decide which receipts you want to keep and can put them right into the check file.

Download Recent Transactions Into Your Financial Software Program

Quicken™, Microsoft Money™, Quickbooks™ and other money managing programs allow you to directly download the recent transactions from your bank into your financial software program. This type of electronic banking ledger allows you to quickly and easily run many types of financial reports.

QuickBooks™ is better for business use as you can print invoices and run payroll with this financial software program. Don't make your finances any more complicated than they have to be. Choose the program that works best for what you need. Be sure that your bank is compatible with the most recent edition of the financial software program that you have.

You can look at monthly or year-to-date expense reports to determine a budget, or to just get an idea of your income versus expenses. These financial software programs are easy to use and have excellent features for determining household spending. Financial software and Internet banking make it easier than ever to manage your money.

Sign Up for
Automatic Bill Paying

This will be one of the greatest time and money savers you have ever done. Automatic bill paying saves you time every month, for every bill. It saves you money because you will never have to use stamps or pay a late fee again. Automatic bill paying also reduces stress because you don't have to worry about when each individual bill is due.

If you are concerned about the security of online bill paying, please know that every major financial institution uses electronic safeguards to protect the privacy and confidentiality of your information. Electronic financial transactions are typically very safe.

Every bank has a different process to sign up for automatic bill paying. Log on to your bank's website and look for an Online Banking button. When you click the Online Banking icon, you will be led to a secure page where you can set up your log-in information. It's fast, it's easy, and it saves you time and money. What isn't to love about automatic bill paying? All you need to do is make sure there is enough money in your account for more than your average monthly expenses.

I highly encourage every monthly household bill, such as phone, utilities, cable, etc., to be an automatically paid bill. The average household receives about 15 bills a month. Stamps are now 41 cents each, so you will save more than $70 per year on postage alone. With automatic bill pay, you save time, money, and reduce stress. Success!

> *"Never give up, for that is just the place and the time that the tide will turn."*
> HARRIET BEECHER STOWE

10-Minute Tidy
TIP 95

Pay Five Bills Right Now

If you don't have all of your bills on automatic bill pay, whether you pay bills online or by handwritten check, you can easily pay five bills in 10 minutes when you are organized. It is very important to keep all of your bills that need to be paid in one place. The "Bills to Be Paid" area could be a file on the top of your desk, in a desk drawer, in a slot in the kitchen, or kept in your briefcase. Wherever you keep your bills to be paid, always put bills there so that you can find all of them quickly and easily.

If you pay bills online, I encourage you to keep your "Bills to Be Paid" next to the computer. That way you can pay all the ones that are currently due in one sitting.

If you pay your bills by writing checks, keep the bills near the checkbook. You will also want to keep a supply of stamps, envelopes and return address labels in this area as well.

If your bills are due at various times throughout the month and you want to simplify your bill paying process even further, call each company and ask for your bills to be due on a more convenient day of the month for you.

Transfer 10 Percent of Your Checking Balance into Savings

It is important to pay yourself first. In today's society of over-consumption, most people buy more of everything than they need. This is how all of the cabinets, closets, and garages fill up with so much stuff! You can not only reduce your stuff but also save for your future.

Take a minimum of 10 percent of your checking balance and transfer it into your savings account right now. Create a plan to save 10 percent of your income: if you receive a regular paycheck, have 10 percent transferred into your savings account and the remainder deposited into your checking account. After a few weeks you will have adopted your lifestyle to the amount available for spending. If 10 percent feels like too much to immediately cut out of your monthly budget, start with 5 percent and gradually work up to 10 percent or more.

You will also save money by switching to a free checking account. With all the banks to choose from, there's no reason to pay a monthly fee. To find the best free checking deals in your local area, go to **www.bankrate.com.** You can save more than $20 in monthly fees by switching banks.

You can also have your savings invested at an institution that offers a higher interest rate to reap the benefits of compound interest. The following websites offer a wide variety of interest-accruing accounts as well as money markets and CDs:

+ E*TRADE **www.etrade.com**

+ Fidelity Investments **www.fidelity.com**

+ **www.bankcd.com**

Start investing in your future today. You deserve it!

"If you would be wealthy,
think of saving as well as getting."
BEN FRANKLIN

Finances

Contribute to a Cause

Money always flows in and flows out and it's important to share with others less fortunate. I have already shared with you about how great it feels to donate the items that you no longer want. Making a financial contribution is another important way to feel better about helping others. Not only can you receive a great tax deduction but you can also feel more generous when making an offering. Check with your tax advisor about filing a "Schedule A" to deduct charitable contributions.

In 10 minutes you could choose which charity or charities to adopt and make a contribution. The Better Business Bureau offers a report on a variety of charities, **www.give.org**. Once you have decided where you would like to contribute, it is easy to set up an automatic monthly deduction to your favorite church, synagogue, or charity. Even $20 per month adds up to a generous sum at the end of the year. Depending on which country the money is allocated for, $20 can purchase enough food to feed a family of four for a month!

If $20 is too much, even $5 per month adds up. As a student, Sharon couldn't contribute a lump sum of $60 to one of her favorite non-commercial radio stations (KQED). Fortunately, they had an option for an automatic deduction of $5 per month, which still added up to $60 per year. This win-win solution event qualified Sharon for a free gift!

If you have several causes or charities you would like to support, but only have a limited amount to extend, give a little to each one. It is said that if the whole U.S. population gave just $1 to each charity, then that would be millions of dollars per year; enough to support a multitude of good causes!

"You will find, as you look back on your life, that the moments that stand out are the moments when you have done things for others."
HENRY DRUMMOND

TIP *98*

Call Your Credit Card Company and Ask for a Lower Interest Rate

Did you know that you can ask for a lower interest rate? Call each credit card customer service line and ask them to lower your interest rate. You will be amazed at how easy this is! If you are not satisfied with the interest rate they offer you, shop around to transfer your balance to another credit card.

Bankrate, **www.bankrate.com**, allows you to search for various credit cards that have particular features you are looking for. You may get better features with a credit card that offers 0% interest or "reward miles" for purchases or balance transfers. There is no reason to be loyal to a credit card that is not willing to work with you.

If you do transfer your balance from one credit card to another, you may still want to keep the older card open to retain your good credit history with them. Long-term credit relations, even if you have a zero balance, improve your credit score. On the other hand, too many open credit cards may work against you by lowering your credit score. Credit scores are described in much greater detail by Suze Ormon, **www.suzeormon.com**.

Garage

"Courage is not the absence of fear.
Courage is taking action in spite of fear."
UNKNOWN

Most American garages are the place where everyone in the family stores all the items they don't know what to do with. Or perhaps they don't know where the item goes in the garage, because there are no designated areas for most items, so things just get stacked on top of stacks of random stuff.

Do you have the goal of being able to park your car in your garage? Maybe even get a second car into the garage? Or perhaps you have offsite storage and you want to be able save the $100+ per month that you have been paying for extra storage, and instead, find space for those items in your garage.

This chapter is devoted to helping you clear the clutter from your garage in small increments so that what appears to be an overwhelming process can be accomplished easily. Begin with whatever seems easiest, perhaps just by the garage entrance or by creating a wider path to the washer and dryer if they are in your garage. Set your timer for 10 minutes. Ready? Set? Go!

Sort and Organize Cleaning Products

Do you store cleaning products in your garage? Most homes have cleaning products under the kitchen sink, in every bathroom, and in the garage. How many of these products do you actually need?

Rather than having 10-20 (or more) bottles of cleaning solutions throughout the house, create a cleaning caddy that has all the basics that you will need, whether you are in the kitchen or bathroom. Broad-spectrum cleaning agents can work for the bathroom countertops as well as the kitchen counters; just use a different cleaning rag or sponge.

I highly recommend using environmentally-friendly cleaning products so that you are not contaminating your home or your skin while cleaning. Simple ingredients work just as well as the fancier, more expensive versions. Gaiam™ is a great company that offers eco-friendly household cleaning products: **www.gaiam.com**. Look at their Home & Outdoor page listing Household Cleaners.

Individual cleaning wipes are a great option if you want to have something in each bathroom and kitchen area for quick cleaning before someone stops by. These disposable wipes are also a quick and easy cleaning option for your kids to wipe up after themselves.

Don't keep cleaning products in the garage if that is not where you will use them. Keep them where you *will* use them. Get rid of anything that you do not use.

Suzanne was moving out of state and the movers would not take any liquids so she had to get rid of more than 40 types of household cleaners. The homeless shelter was so grateful to receive all of her cleaning supplies that they will now use in their family center. Give away your extra cleaning supplies and let others benefit from the things you do not need. What is great about donating unwanted cleaning supplies is that this keeps these chemicals out of the landfill or from being poured down the drain.

TIP 100

Install a Mop and Broom Hanging System

Do you use your mop and then stick it back in some corner while it's still wet? For less than $10 you can purchase a mop and broom hanging system from a hardware store. This 16"-20" track is easily mounted on the wall using two or three screws and has 4-6 clips on it that you can use to hang up your mop, broom, dust pan, feather duster and whatever else easily snaps into place. This is a great way to get your cleaning tools off the floor, and easily separated for a quick grab when you need each one.

Using a stationary, mounted hanging system empowers everyone to know where these cleaning tools are kept and where they need to be returned. Only keep what you use and donate the rest. I had a client who had five brooms in her home. Do you need five brooms?

While you are at the hardware store you may want to see what else is available. For example, there may be a similar system for you to hang your ironing board. This also saves floor space and prevents the ironing board from accidentally falling over if it is bumped.

TIP 101

Organize the Shelf Above the Washer and Dryer

Wherever your washer and dryer are, there is usually a shelf right above them. The stackable washer and dryers are great for space-saving and they also save you the chore of clearing off the shelf above them. You can skip this one if you have a stackable washer and dryer!

The shelf above or next to the washer and dryer tends to get sticky from drips of laundry detergent and dusty from dryer lint. For this area, I encourage you to take everything off, wipe the shelf down and only put back what you will use. Get rid of or donate all those sample packs, or put them with your travel stuff if you will use them while traveling.

Group your detergents and fabric softeners over the washer and keep the dryer sheets above the dryer. Anything else you store on this shelf should be easy to see and grab. Paper towels are a good idea for wiping up laundry detergent drips and spills. Keep the area around your washer and dryer clean and spacious for better ventilation. If you have any time left during this 10-Minute Tidy, you could even vacuum around the washer and dryer.

Straighten Up the Workbench

My client Jeff and I spent a Saturday morning straightening up his workbench and it has made a huge difference in his ability to make home repairs. You can start to organize your workbench area in 10-minute increments by focusing on just one area.

Start with the basic tools. Organize them so that the hammer is always in a place close to the nails and picture hooks. Have the screws stored near the screwdrivers. Can your tape measure be found within a few second's glance at the workbench? Better yet, for quick access to everything, have all your basic household tools in a handled bucket or toolbox.

It's important to be able to step up to your workbench and have a clear area to set down anything that you are going to work on. Bright lighting is also necessary for seeing the heads of screws, the size of drill bits and the exact measurement of something that needs to be cut.

Pegboards are a common way to hang up a variety of tools. I have also seen walls where the tool that hangs there has been outlined so that it is very obvious what gets hung where and all excuses for not returning something to its proper place are eliminated.

Once you have spent time straightening up the workbench, it is very easy to tidy every time you use it.

"*Organizing is what you do before you do something, so that when you do it, it's not all mixed up.*"
A.A. MILNE

TIP 103

Sort One Box in Your Garage

I love this quote by Yoda: "Do or do not. There is no try." You have to decide to sort one box in your garage. Until you decide to do it, the boxes will stay piled up. Perhaps you still have boxes from when you moved into your home. How long ago was that? If you have lived without the items in that box for more than six months, chances are you don't really need to keep anything in the box.

Ask yourself why you have been avoiding unpacking or even opening the boxes in the garage. If there is stuff in those boxes with lots of negative energy, such as from a divorce, a previous job or a deceased relative, consider why you are keeping the box at all. I highly encourage and support you to get rid of anything that has negative memories associated with it. You get to keep your own memories in your mind; you don't need to keep physical reminders around too.

If you do feel like it is important to keep boxes that will be accessed very infrequently, then put them high up, and as far back in your garage as you can so that the boxes that you do need regular access to are more available. Keeping boxes higher up also helps reduce damage from mold, mildew, and flooding. Transferring items into plastic bins with tight-fitting lids will also greatly reduce the damage caused by moisture, insects and rodents.

Set a timer for 10 minutes and see how much you can eliminate from one box only. Is there anything to donate in this box? Are there any packing materials to recycle? What can go into the house right away? What did you find that you were missing? Have each box be a treasure chest just waiting to be opened!

"Attempt the impossible in order to improve your work."
BETTIE DAVIS

Sort and Hang Gardening Tools

In most climates, gardening tools are used seasonally. Having your gardening tools sorted and stored for easy access makes this hobby much more enjoyable. So, get your timer and set it for 10 minutes.

Designate one area of your garage or shed to gardening so that everyone can get the gloves, seeds, pots or tools that they might need for planting, maintaining or harvesting from the garden. At the beginning of the season, take stock of what you have, what condition your tools are in, and what you may want to purchase. I know right where the trowel is stored in our garage, so if I get a spontaneous urge to buy a 6-pack of flowers, I know that I can come home and plant them quickly and easily.

Get rid of any pesticides or fertilizers that have expired or were damaged during the winter. Please be responsible and dispose of your pesticides and other chemicals properly, or better yet, only use organic products.

Enjoy gardening even more by having your gardening supplies organized and easy to use.

Organize Sports Equipment by Season

Sports equipment is seasonal, expensive, and will last much longer if it is stored properly. Now you have the opportunity to check out your sports equipment and see what you have and how to store it better. Is your timer set to 10?

Organize particular equipment by sport so that the biking gloves and helmets are kept near the bikes. Bins or boxes that contain the various pieces of equipment that you will use with each sport keep items together so that they are easier to find. Have the tennis racquets stored with the tennis balls. Skis need proper storage so that they will not fall over during the months that they are not used.

Home Organization Solutions™, **www.orghomesolutions. com**, and Budget Closet™, **www.budgetcloset.com**, offer great ways to organize the sports equipment in your garage. Choose storage solutions that will suit your needs best.

If you want to keep your golf clubs closer to the front of the garage so that they are easy to put in the trunk of your car, clear an area along the wall where the golf bag can be propped up. Be sure to empty out the pockets of your golf bag at the end of the season. Bob left sunflower seeds in the pocket and when we cleaned out the garage, it was obvious that a mouse had eaten a hole in his bag and found his stash!

Properly storing your sports equipment will make it more accessible and easier to use whenever you choose.

"If you worried about falling off the bike, you'd never get on."
LANCE ARMSTRONG

Organize the Glove Box

It's amazing what we can cram into the smallest areas! The glove box is the car's catch all for maps, tissues, and maybe a flashlight if you're lucky. What's jammed into the glove box of your car? In the next 10 minutes, you can organize this one area.

I recommend you put the most important documents for your car into a plastic holder: something easy to find in a hurry. The owner's manual usually comes in a plastic holder, so this is a common place to store your insurance and registration. You don't want to be sorting through lots of napkins, calculators, pens, and other items when you really need your proof of insurance and registration.

Keren uses a plastic accordion check file with seven sections labeled: Registration, Insurance, Car Wash Coupons, Local Maps, Driving Directions, National Maps, and Misc. This keeps all of her papers contained and leaves other space for an extra pair of sunglasses, sunscreen, mini-flashlight and a snack bar.

Organizing the glove box ensures that you have all the necessary papers and tools stored for quick and easy access.

Designate a Trash Bin
for Your Car

Having a designated trash bag or bin in my car has made it quick and easy for me to clean out my car while I'm filling my gas tank. Rather than having to rummage beneath and between all the seats to find old apple cores and used tissues, I now just have a bag behind the passenger seat that I can easily reach and discard whatever I need to.

Auto supply stores have several types of trash bag options to choose from. Some mount to the back of the car seat, others stand up between bucket seats. Re-using a plastic grocery bag as the designated car garbage bag is free, quick and very easy. It can hang over your gear shifter, hook over a manual window handle, or just sit on the floor. I have found that a sturdy plastic bag is better than something flimsy, but plastic grocery bags will work just fine. You decide what is best for your vehicle.

Putting a designated trash bag in each vehicle will only take a few minutes. While the timer is ticking, you could clean out the old trash stuck under the seats and take pleasure in doing this for the very last time!

Celebrate Your Successfully Organized Home!

"Success is the sum of small efforts,
repeated day in and day out."
ROBERT COLLIER

CONGRATULATIONS! You have learned many ways to quickly and easily keep your home more organized. Only you can change your habits and practice these tips. You have the power and I know you can do it! I celebrate your successes; share your stories with me.

I wish you grace, ease, abundance and joy in all that you do! Ready? Set? GO CELEBRATE!

"Desire is the key to motivation,
but it's the determination and commitment
to an unrelenting pursuit of your goal
—a commitment to excellence—
that will enable you to attain the success you seek."
TOM TOGNOLI

Appendix A
Get Rid of Junk Mail Forever

1. Online: **www.stopjunk.com** or **www.dmaconsumers.org**

2. Call: National Opt-Out Center: 1-888-567-8688

3. Write: Direct Marketing Association
Mail Preference Service
PO Box 282
Carmel, NY 10512

Online form at **www.dmaconsumers.org/mailform.php**

Your sample letter should state: "I want to reduce the amount of unsolicited mail I receive. Please remove my name and address from your mailing list." Include all variations of your name: Bob Smith, Robert Smith, B. Smith, etc. with your Name, Address, City, State, Zip, and Signature.

This is well worth your time!

Appendix B
Save It or Shred It?

Keep for 1 month:
- All receipts for potential returning of items
- Withdrawal and deposit slips
  (Shred these after reconciling monthly bank statement)

Keep for 1 year:
- Paycheck stubs
- Monthly bank, credit card, brokerage, mutual fund, and retirement account statements

Keep for 7 years:
- Tax returns, W-2s, 1099s, etc.
- Any tax-supporting or related documents
- Year-end credit card statements, brokerage, and mutual fund summaries

Keep indefinitely:

• Receipts for major purchases

• Real estate records

• Wills and Trusts

What to store in your safe deposit or fire-proof box:

• Birth certificates

• Bonds and stock certificates

• Social security cards

• Passports

• Insurance policies

• Vehicle titles

• Wills and Trusts

• Property deeds

• Marriage, business and professional licenses

Other important items to consider:

• College diplomas

• School transcripts

• Old tax returns

Be sure to photocopy or scan each of these important documents before you store them. Read **Tip 80** for more details about these documents.

Appendix C
Hire a Professional Organizer

Professional Organizers can help you create order out of your chaos. What is your situation right now? How would you like it to be? What do you want help with? Any organizing job will get done faster and be easier if you hire a professional to help you rather than trying to sort through everything by yourself.

A Professional Organizer will share organizing tools and strategies with you and the project will be more fun. Visit the National Association of Professional Organizers, **www.napo. net**, to learn more about how a Professional Organizer can help you. You can also hire a professional organizer in your local area by using NAPO's automated referral program.

All NAPO members are held to a strict code of ethics and are wonderful resources for support and transformation. We look forward to working with you and all of the people in your life who would like to be more organized!

Acknowledgements

"Success is a journey, not a destination."
BEN SWEETLAND

This book has been an amazing creative birthing process for me. I would not have been able to share my expertise with you if not for the strong support of my clients, friends, and colleagues.

Writing a book is a collaboration of many people. Thank you Sharon Evans for being a fantastic editor. Thank you Ian Webb for formatting this book and fine tuning the details. Huge thanks to Scott Evans of Creative Resource Group for the final book cover and website.

The mothers in my life provided their stories and strategies for keeping their families organized. Thank you: Gwendolyn, Grace, Denise, Maia, Tanya, April and Allyson.

My girlfriends offered immense support. Thank you: Keren, Carla, Talya, Tricia, Gwendolyn, Karrie, Grace, Katie, Elizabeth and Sarah. I love and adore each of you.

My best friend and partner Scott has been a wonderful reminder of commitment, love and support.

Thank you all so very much!

Index

Index

Index

Index

Index

What To Do Next

If you would like more information about *The 10-Minute Tidy* or other organizing products and services we have developed, please check out our website at **www.10minutetidy.com.**

There you will find information on:

- Free organizing newsletter with tidying tips

- How to attend a "10-Minute Tidy" or "Key Strategies for Being Organized 4 Success!" seminar

- How to hire Shannon McGinnis to speak at your next event

- Instructional DVDs

- Downloadable seminar, transcripts, and handouts

- Instructional CDs and workbook

- Coming soon…Shannon's next book: ***The 10-Minute Tidy in the Office***

To everyone who has called and emailed me…THANK YOU SO VERY MUCH! I am incredibly grateful. If this book has made a significant impact on you, please let me know about your successes!

About The Author

Shannon McGinnis is a Certified Professional Organizer, author, and consultant. Shannon is founder of Organized 4 Success, a company dedicated to simplifying the way people organize their homes and offices. As one of the nations first Certified Professional Organizers, Shannon offers her clients expert advice on a variety of topics such as space management, time management, and general organizing principles. She has been featured on radio programs and is a popular speaker around the country. Shannon is the creator of the "Key Strategies for Being Organized 4 Success!" seminar series from which thousands of people have benefited by learning easy-to-implement organizing strategies.

Shannon lives near Santa Cruz, California. Visit her online at **www.10minutetidy.com** and **www.organized4success.com**.

"Out of clutter, find simplicity;
from discord, find harmony;
in the middle of difficulty lies opportunity."
ALBERT EINSTEIN